Contents

Pamphlet Series   No. 45 Sixth Edition

Financial Organization and Operations of the IMF

Treasurer's Department

INTERNATIONAL MONETARY FUND
Washington, D.C.
2001

ISSN 0538-8759
ISBN 1-58906-067-9
Sixth Edition, 2001

Please send orders to:
International Monetary Fund, Publication Services
700 19th Street, N.W., Washington, D.C. 20431, U.S.A.
Tel.: (202) 623-7430   Telefax: (202) 623-7201
E-mail: publications@imf.org
Internet: http://www.imf.org

Tables

Figures

Unless indicated otherwise, statistical information is given for financial year 2001, which began May 1, 2000 and ended April 30, 2001. Current financial information is available on the IMF's website (www.imf.org/external/fin.htm). The following conventions have been used in this pamphlet:

n.a. to indicate not applicable;

...   to indicate that data are not available;

—   to indicate that the figure is zero or less than half the final digit shown or that the item does not exist;

( )   to indicate that the figure is negative;

–   between years or months (for example, 2000–01, or January–June) to indicate the years or months covered, including the beginning and ending years or months;

/   between years or months (for example, 2000/01) to indicate a fiscal or financial year.

"Billion" means a thousand million; "trillion" means a thousand billion.

"Basis points" refer to hundredths of 1 percentage point (for example, 25 basis points are equivalent to ¼ of 1 percentage point).

Minor discrepancies between constituent figures and totals are due to rounding.

All references to dollars are to U.S. dollars unless otherwise indicated; as of April 30, 2001, the SDR/U.S. dollar exchange rate was US$1 = SDR 0.790019, and the U.S. dollar/SDR exchange rate was SDR 1 = US$1.26579.

As used in this pamphlet, the term "country" does not in all cases refer to a territorial entity that is a state as understood by international law and practice. As used here, the term also covers some territorial entities that are not states but for which statistical data are maintained on a separate and independent basis.

Preface

This extensively revised edition of the pamphlet *Financial Organization and Operations of the IMF* is part of a broader effort to improve the transparency of all of the IMF's financial activities. The IMF's new financial statements, conforming fully with International Accounting Standards, are used in this pamphlet to present the financial operations in a generally recognized framework. The IMF's external website contains current information on all elements of the IMF's financial activities (www.imf.org/external/fin.htm) and is used widely by the interested public. This pamphlet provides the context and analytical background to the information on the website.

This new edition has been prepared by staff members of the Treasurer's Department under the direction of Michael Wattleworth, Advisor. I would also like to acknowledge the valuable contribution of colleagues in the Policy Development and Review, Legal, and External Relations Departments. The views expressed in this pamphlet, including any legal aspects, are those of the IMF staff and should not be attributed to Executive Directors of the IMF or their national authorities.

This edition is current as of spring 2001. The pamphlet will be updated as warranted.

EDUARD BRAU
Treasurer
International Monetary Fund

Abbreviations

BIS	Bank for International Settlements
CFF	Compensatory Financing Facility
CCL	Contingent Credit Line
EAC	External Audit Committee
EAP	Enlarged Access Policy
EFF	Extended Fund Facility
ESAF	Enhanced Structural Adjustment Facility
FSAP	Financial Sector Assessment Program
GAB	General Arrangements to Borrow
GDDS	General Data Dissemination System
GRA	General Resources Account
HIPC	Heavily Indebted Poor Countries
IAS	International Accounting Standards
IDA	International Development Association
IMFC	International Monetary and Financial Committee
ISA	International Standards on Auditing
MTI	Medium-Term Instrument
NAB	New Arrangements to Borrow
NPV	Net Present Value
OPEC	Organization of the Petroleum Exporting Countries
PIN	Public Information Notice
PRGF	Poverty Reduction and Growth Facility
PRSP	Poverty Reduction Strategy Paper
QFRG	Quota Formula Review Group
RAP	Rights Accumulation Program
ROSC	Report on the Observance of Standards and Codes
SAF	Structural Adjustment Facility
SAMA	Saudi Arabian Monetary Agency
SCA	Special Contingent Account
SDA	Special Disbursement Account
SDDS	Special Data Dissemination Standard
SDR	Special Drawing Right
SRF	Supplemental Reserve Facility

I

Overview of the IMF as a Financial Institution

Role and Purposes of the IMF

The International Monetary Fund is a cooperative international monetary organization whose members currently include 183 countries of the world. It was established together with the World Bank in 1945 as part of the Bretton Woods conference convened in the aftermath of World War II.

The responsibilities of the IMF derive from the basic purposes for which the institution was established, as set out in Article I of the IMF Articles of Agreement — the charter that governs all policies and activities of the IMF:

- To promote international cooperation through a permanent institution which provides the machinery for consultation and collaboration on international monetary problems.

- To facilitate the expansion and balanced growth of international trade, and to contribute thereby to the promotion and maintenance of high levels of employment and real income and to the development of the productive resources of all members as primary objectives of economic policy.

- To promote exchange stability, to maintain orderly exchange arrangements among members, and to avoid competitive exchange depreciation.

- To assist in the establishment of a multilateral system of payments in respect of current transactions between members and in the elimination of foreign exchange restrictions which hamper the growth of world trade.

- To give confidence to members by making the general resources of the Fund temporarily available to them under adequate safeguards, thus providing them with opportunity to correct maladjustments in their balance of payments without resorting to measures destructive of national or international prosperity.

- In accordance with the above, to shorten the duration and lessen the degree of disequilibrium in the international balances of payments of members.

The IMF is best known as a financial institution that provides resources to member countries experiencing temporary balance of payments problems on the condition that the borrower undertake economic adjustment policies to address these difficulties. In recent years, IMF lending increased dramatically as the institution played a central role in resolving a series of economic and financial crises in emerging market countries in Asia, Latin America, and Europe. The IMF is also actively engaged in promoting economic growth and poverty reduction in its poorer members by providing financing on concessional terms in support of efforts to stabilize economies, implement structural reforms, and achieve sustainable external debt positions. Often missing from the public perception of the IMF, however, is the broader context in which this financing takes place.

The IMF is unique among intergovernmental organizations in its combination of regulatory, consultative, and financial functions, which derive from the purposes for which the institution was established.[1] Supporting the IMF's legal mandate are a variety of voluntary service and informational functions that facilitate the implementation of its official tasks:

- *Regulatory functions* of the IMF include formal jurisdiction over measures that have the effect of restricting payments and transfers for current international transactions. Member countries are required to provide the IMF with such information and statistical data as it deems necessary for its activities, including the minimum necessary for the effective discharge of its duties, as outlined in the Articles of Agreement (Article VIII).

- *Consultative functions* stem primarily from the IMF's responsibility for overseeing the international monetary system and exercising firm surveillance over the policies of its members, a task entrusted to the IMF following the collapse of the Bretton Woods fixed exchange rate system in the early 1970s.[2] These activities include regular monitoring and peer review by other members of economic and financial developments and policies in each of its members under Article IV of the Articles of Agreement, ongoing reviews of world economic and financial market

---

[1]See Manuel Guitián, *The Unique Nature of the Responsibilities of the International Monetary Fund,* IMF Pamphlet Series No. 46 (Washington: International Monetary Fund, 1992).

[2]See the discussion in Chapter III for an explanation of how the fixed exchange rate system worked.

developments, and semiannual consideration of the world economic outlook (Article IV).

- *Financial functions* of the IMF are the subject of this pamphlet. They range from the provision of temporary balance of payments financing and administration of the SDR system to the extension of longer-term concessional lending and debt relief to the poorest members (Articles V and VI).

- *Service and supplementary informational functions* are voluntary, in contrast to the obligatory nature of members' participation in the above three areas of the IMF operations. These supportive functions include a wide-ranging program of technical assistance and encompass an array of statistical and nonstatistical activities, most notably the collection and dissemination of economic and financial data on its member countries, reporting on its country and global surveillance assessments, and disseminating its policy and research findings. In many cases, the IMF is the chief source of reliable, up-to-date economic information on individual countries. Increasingly, the institution is also called on by its members to develop and monitor adherence to standards and best practices in several areas, including timely country economic and financial statistics, monetary and fiscal transparency, the assessment of financial sector soundness, and the promotion of good governance.

The IMF is therefore concerned not only with the problems of individual countries but also with the working of the international monetary system as a whole. Its activities are aimed at promoting policies and strategies through which its members can work together to ensure a stable world financial system and sustainable economic growth. The IMF provides a forum for international monetary cooperation, and thus for an orderly evolution of the system, and it subjects a wide area of international monetary affairs to the covenants of law, moral suasion, and understandings. The IMF must also stand ready to deal with crisis situations, not only those affecting individual members but also those representing threats to the international monetary system.

All operations of the IMF are conducted under a decision-making structure that has evolved over the years (Box I.1). The governance structure attempts to strike a balance between universal representation and the operational necessities of managing an effective financial institution. While every member country is represented separately on the Board of Governors, most

---

BOX I.1. DECISION-MAKING STRUCTURE OF THE IMF

The IMF has a Board of Governors, an Executive Board, a Managing Director, and a staff of nearly 3,000 that roughly reflects the diversity of its membership. The Board of Governors is the highest policymaking body of the IMF; it consists of one Governor and one Alternate appointed by each member. The Board of Governors, whose members are usually ministers of finance, heads of central banks, or officials of comparable rank, normally meets once a year.

An International Monetary and Financial Committee (IMFC), currently composed of 24 IMF Governors, ministers, or others of comparable rank (reflecting the composition of the Executive Board and representing all IMF members), usually meets twice a year. This committee advises and reports to the Board of Governors on the management and functioning of the international monetary system, proposals by the Executive Board to amend the Articles of Agreement, and any sudden disturbances that might threaten the system. A committee with a similar composition, the Development Committee, maintains an overview of the development process and reports to the Board of Governors of the World Bank and the IMF and makes suggestions on all aspects of the broad question of the transfer of resources to developing countries.

The IMF Executive Board is responsible for conducting the business of the IMF and exercises the powers delegated to it by the Board of Governors. It functions in continuous session at IMF headquarters and currently consists of 24 Executive Directors, with the Managing Director (or one of the three Deputy Managing Directors acting for the Managing Director) as the Chairman. The Managing Director is selected by the Executive Board and is the chief of the operating staff of the IMF. The three Deputy Managing Directors are appointed by the Managing Director with the approval of the Executive Board.

The number of votes that a member can cast is related to the size of its quota at the IMF. The five members with the largest quotas each appoint their Executive Directors, as can the two members with the largest creditor positions in the IMF over the two years preceding an election if these members are not part of the group of the five largest members. The remaining Directors are elected from among the other member countries that may form themselves into groups or constituencies. A number of important decisions specified in the Articles of Agreement require either 70 percent or 85 percent of the total voting power; other decisions are made by a majority of the votes cast.

---

members form combined constituencies on the much smaller Executive Board that conducts the day-to-day business of the IMF. While voting power is based on the size of capital subscriptions, giving the greatest voice to the institution's largest contributors, smaller members are protected with a fixed number of basic votes. Moreover, the Executive Board takes most decisions based on consensus, without a formal vote.

This pamphlet aims to explain the IMF's financial organization and operations—that is, how the IMF works as a financial institution, focusing on its financial structure as of the spring of 2001, but including enough background information to make that structure understandable.

Evolution of the IMF's Financial Structure

The single most important feature of the financial structure of the IMF is that it is continuously developing. This is necessary for the IMF to meet the needs of an ever-changing global economic and financial system.

The IMF has introduced and refined a variety of lending facilities and policy changes over the years to address changing conditions in the global economy or the specific circumstances of members.[3] It discontinued or modified such adaptations when the need for them was reduced or eliminated.

- During 1945–60, the IMF facilitated the move to convertibility among countries for current payments and the removal of restrictions on trade and payments that had been put in place before and during the war. This was also a period of relatively low financing by the IMF, as the Marshall Plan of the United States largely assumed that role.

- During 1961–70, to meet the pressures on the Bretton Woods fixed exchange rate system, the IMF developed a new supplementary reserve asset (the special drawing right, or SDR) and a standing borrowing arrangement with the largest creditor members to supplement its resources during times of systemic crisis.

- During 1971–80, the two world oil crises led to an expansion of IMF financing and the development of new lending facilities funded from borrowed resources. The decade also marked the IMF's expansion into concessional lending to its poorest members.

---

[3]The provision of financial assistance by the IMF is not technically or legally "lending" as such. Rather, financial assistance is provided via an exchange of monetary assets, similar to a swap. Nevertheless, the purchase and repurchase of currencies from the IMF, with interest charged on outstanding purchases, is functionally equivalent to a loan and its subsequent repayment, as explained in Chapter II (see Box II.1). Accordingly, for ease of reference, the terms "lending," "loans," and "borrowing" are used in this pamphlet to refer to the provision of financial resources by the IMF to its members.

- During 1981–90, the developing country debt crisis triggered a further sharp increase in IMF financing, with higher levels of assistance to individual countries, again financed in part by borrowed resources.

- During 1991–2000, the IMF established a temporary lending facility to facilitate the integration of the formerly centrally planned economies into the world market system. The globalization of financial markets also required adaptation of the financing facilities designed for an earlier era when current account imbalances predominated to a world in which large and sudden shifts in international capital flows resulted in payments imbalances originating in the capital account.

Following a major review of its lending policies and facilities in 2000, the IMF introduced a number of important changes to encourage early adoption of sound economic policies as a means of preventing crises and to reduce excessively long or large-scale use of its resources. Looking ahead, the challenge is to design and implement tools to assist members in the early detection of financial crises.

Most of the developments described above were accommodated through policy changes in the IMF's regular lending operations, within the original financial structure that was created at the Bretton Woods conference. This structure reflected the IMF's basic purpose of financing short-term payments imbalances between member countries under the fixed exchange rate system created after World War II. Since capital markets were not integrated at that time, these payments imbalances arose from trade and other current transactions among countries. The financial mechanism designed to fulfill this purpose is in the General Department of IMF, specifically the General Resources Account, or GRA.

The financing mechanism of the GRA continues to function much as it was originally designed. But the number of members that provide resources for the IMF's financial operations has expanded from early reliance on the United States and the major European countries to an ever wider array of members whose balance of payments positions became strong enough to support IMF lending. In mid-2001, there were 38 countries financing IMF assistance through the GRA. As the group of IMF creditor countries continued to widen, the countries borrowing from the IMF also shifted from largely the industrial countries in the IMF's first 25 years to the developing and emerging market countries in the last 25 years.

Although most developments in the world economic system could be accommodated through changes in the IMF's lending policies implemented through the GRA, two major transformations resulted in lasting changes in the financial structure of the IMF:

- First, the creation of special drawing rights (SDRs) in 1969 and establishment in the IMF of a separate SDR Department to conduct all operations in SDRs. The Bretton Woods fixed exchange rate system came under pressure during the 1960s because it contained no mechanism for regulating reserve growth to finance the expansion of world trade and financial development. Gold production was an inadequate and unreliable source of reserve supply and the continuing growth in U.S. dollar reserves required a persistent deficit in the U.S. balance of payments, which itself posed a threat to the value of the U.S. dollar. The solution to the reserve problem lay in creating an international reserve asset to supplement dollars and gold in official reserve holdings. The creation of the SDR was intended to make the regulation of international liquidity, for the first time, subject to international consultation and decision. Only a few years after the creation of the SDR, however, the Bretton Woods system collapsed and the major currencies shifted to a floating exchange rate regime. This, along with the growth in international capital markets and the expanded capacity of creditworthy governments to borrow, lessened the need for SDRs.

- Second, the involvement of the IMF in providing financial assistance on concessional terms to the IMF's poorest members beginning in the late 1970s.[4] This fundamental shift recognized that the IMF's poorest members required different terms of financing and had different policy requirements than did the rest of the membership in adjusting to external imbalances. Since the IMF's legal structure does not permit lending on concessional terms, the concessional operations are conducted under administered accounts, with the IMF acting in the capacity of Trustee of the resources. During 1976–86, concessional lending was financed by selling a portion of the IMF's gold holdings. The level of lending was initially relatively low, with few policy conditions attached

---

[4]Concessional terms are those that are below the IMF's marginal cost of funds, which, as explained later, is linked to short-term interest rates prevailing in the world's four largest money markets.

to the loans. Beginning in 1987, the volume of concessional finance expanded sharply, subject to higher levels of conditionality, with financing provided through borrowed resources, grants for subsidized interest rates and debt relief, and repayments of past concessional loans.

Current Financial Structure and Lending Mechanisms of the IMF

The IMF provides financing to its members through three channels, all of which have the common purpose of transferring reserve currencies to member countries. In both its regular and concessional lending operations, financing is provided primarily under "arrangements" with the IMF, which are similar to lines of credit. For the large majority of IMF lending, use of these lines of credit is conditional upon the achievement of economic stabilization and structural reform objectives agreed between the borrowing member and the IMF. The IMF can also create international reserve assets by allocating SDRs to members, which can be used to obtain foreign exchange from other members. Use of SDRs is unconditional, although a market-based interest rate is charged.

The basic financial structure of the IMF is summarized in Box I.2, which includes references to the relevant chapters of this pamphlet where each of the three financing channels is discussed in detail, and a final chapter that describes the safeguards for IMF resources. The pamphlet is organized on both an institutional and a chronological basis. Summary descriptions of Chapters II–V follow.

Regular Lending Operations (Chapter II)

Unlike other international financial institutions (such as the World Bank or the regional development banks), the IMF is, in effect, a repository for its members' currencies and a portion of their foreign exchange reserves. The IMF uses this pool of currencies and reserve assets to extend credits to member countries when they face economic difficulties as reflected in their external balance of payments.

The IMF's regular lending is financed from the fully paid-in capital subscribed by member countries. It is conducted through the GRA of the General Department, which holds the capital subscribed by members. A country's capital subscription is equal to its IMF quota. Upon joining, each

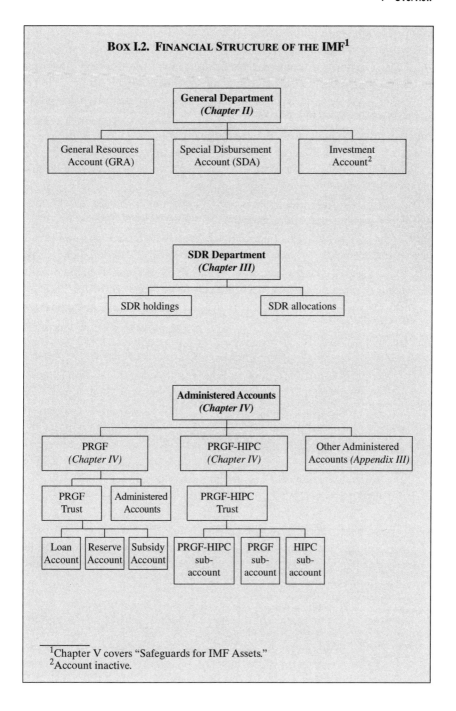

BOX I.2. FINANCIAL STRUCTURE OF THE IMF[1]

General Department
(Chapter II)

General Resources
Account (GRA)

Special Disbursement
Account (SDA)

Investment
Account[2]

SDR Department
(Chapter III)

SDR holdings

SDR allocations

Administered Accounts
(Chapter IV)

PRGF
(Chapter IV)

PRGF-HIPC
(Chapter IV)

Other Administered
Accounts *(Appendix III)*

PRGF
Trust

Administered
Accounts

PRGF-HIPC
Trust

Loan
Account

Reserve
Account

Subsidy
Account

PRGF-HIPC
sub-
account

PRGF
sub-
account

HIPC
sub-
account

[1]Chapter V covers "Safeguards for IMF Assets."
[2]Account inactive.

9

country is assigned a quota that is broadly based on its relative position in the world economy and represents its maximum financial commitment to the IMF.[5] The member country provides a portion of its quota subscription in the form of reserve assets (foreign currencies acceptable to the IMF or SDRs) and the remainder in its own currency. This "reserve position" is made instantly available to a member if the member has a balance of payments need. For its lending the IMF utilizes the reserve assets it already holds and calls on countries that are considered financially strong to exchange the IMF's holdings of their currency for reserve assets that are then made available to borrowing countries.

The bulk of IMF lending is provided under short-term "Stand-By"Arrangements that address balance of payments difficulties of a temporary or cyclical nature. This financing can be supplemented with additional short-term resources to assist members experiencing a sudden and disruptive loss of capital market access. The IMF also lends under medium-term Extended Arrangements that focus on external payments difficulties arising from longer-term structural problems. All credit outstanding incurs interest at the IMF's basic rate of charge, which is based on market interest rates, and can be subject to surcharges depending on the type and duration of the loan and the amount of IMF credit outstanding.

IMF lending is normally conditional on a country adopting and implementing a program of economic reforms affecting major macroeconomic variables such as the exchange rate, money and credit, and the fiscal deficit. Moreover, the financing provided by the IMF is temporary, to be repaid when macroeconomic imbalances have been rectified, and economic performance has improved, so that it may be available for others to use subsequently, thus evoking the analogy of the IMF as an "international credit union."[6]

The IMF's quota-based funds can be supplemented by borrowing under two standing borrowing arrangements, the New Arrangements to Borrow (NAB) and the General Arrangements to Borrow (GAB). If necessary, the IMF can also undertake further borrowing from official sources or private markets to supplement available resources, but to date it has never borrowed from private sources.

---

[5]Quotas also determine a country's voting power in the IMF, generally provide the basis for access to IMF financing, and determine shares in SDR allocations.

[6]Repayment schedules vary according to the specific lending program or "facility," which is designed to address the particular type of balance of payments problems facing the country.

SDR Mechanism (Chapter III)

The SDR is a reserve asset created by the IMF and allocated to participating members in proportion to their IMF quotas to meet a long-term global need to supplement existing reserve assets. A member may use SDRs to obtain foreign exchange reserves from other members and to make international payments, including to the IMF. The SDR is not a currency, nor is it a liability of the IMF, rather it is primarily a potential claim on freely usable currencies. Freely usable currencies, as determined by the IMF, are the U.S. dollar, euro, Japanese yen, and pound sterling. Members are allocated SDRs unconditionally and may use them to obtain freely usable currencies in order to meet a balance of payments financing need without undertaking economic policy measures or repayment obligations. A member that makes net use of its allocated SDRs pays the SDR interest rate on the amount used, while a member that acquires SDRs in excess of its allocation receives the SDR interest rate on its excess holdings. Thus far, the IMF has allocated a total of SDR 21.4 billion.

A special, one-time equity allocation of SDRs that would double the amount of SDRs outstanding is now pending final approval by the membership. The purpose of this allocation is to address a perceived inequity that more than one-fifth of IMF members have never received an SDR allocation because they joined after the last allocation. Provisions have been made for future new members to receive equal treatment.

The SDR serves as the unit of account for the IMF and the SDR interest rate provides the basis for calculating the interest charges on regular IMF financing and the interest rate paid to members that are creditors to the IMF.

- The value of the SDR is based on a basket of currencies, comprising the U.S. dollar, euro, Japanese yen, and pound sterling, and is determined daily based on exchange rates quoted on the major international currency markets.

- The SDR interest rate is determined weekly based on the same currency amounts as in the SDR valuation basket, prevailing exchange rates, and representative interest rates on short-term financial instruments in the markets of the currencies included in the valuation basket.

All SDR transactions are conducted through the SDR Department of the IMF. The SDR is solely an official asset. SDRs are held largely by member countries with the balance held in the IMF's GRA and by official entities prescribed by the IMF to hold SDRs. Neither prescribed holders nor the

IMF receive SDR allocations but can acquire and use SDRs in transactions with IMF members and with other prescribed holders under the same terms and conditions as IMF members.

Concessional Financing (Chapter IV)

The IMF lends to poor countries at an interest rate of ½ of 1 percent and over a longer repayment period than nonconcessional IMF lending while these countries restructure their economies to promote growth and reduce poverty. The IMF also provides assistance on a grant (no-cost) basis to heavily indebted poor countries to help them achieve sustainable external debt positions. These activities are undertaken separately from the IMF's regular lending operations, with resources provided voluntarily by members independently of their IMF capital subscriptions, and in part from the IMF's own resources. The IMF's concessional assistance is extended through the Poverty Reduction and Growth Facility (PRGF) Trust and in the context of the Heavily Indebted Poor Country (HIPC) Initiative through the PRGF-HIPC Trust, both of which the IMF operates as Trustee.

The financing for the IMF's concessional lending and debt relief is mobilized through a cooperative effort currently involving 94 countries. The principal for PRGF loans has in most cases been provided through bilateral lenders at market-based interest rates. This loan principal is passed through to PRGF-eligible borrowers on concessional terms. The financing needed to make up the difference between the concessional interest rate paid by PRGF borrowers and the market-based rate received by PRGF lenders is provided through bilateral contributions and by the IMF from its own resources. The debt relief provided under the HIPC Initiative is also financed from contributions from IMF members and the institution itself.

The framework for the PRGF envisages commitments under the current PRGF Trust through late 2001 or early 2002, to be followed by a four-year interim PRGF with a commitment capacity of about SDR 1 billion a year. The continuation of concessional lending for the period after 2005 will be financed through resources accumulating in the PRGF Reserve Account from repayment of earlier concessional loans and the investment return on these funds. Since the resources in the Reserve Account belong to the IMF, there would be no need for further bilateral loan resources or subsidy contributions. The self-sustained PRGF will have the resources to lend in perpetuity, thus making concessional lending a permanent feature of the IMF's financial structure.

Until needed, PRGF and HIPC resources are invested and the investment income is used to help meet the financial requirements of the PRGF and HIPC initiatives. In March 2000, the IMF put in place a new investment strategy for the resources supporting these initiatives with the objective of supplementing returns over time while maintaining prudent limits on risk.

Safeguards for IMF Resources (Chapter V)

The Articles of Agreement require the IMF to adopt policies that will establish adequate safeguards for the temporary use of the organization's resources. These safeguards can be divided into those aimed at protecting currently available or outstanding credit and those focused on limiting the duration of, and clearing, overdue obligations.

Safeguards to protect committed and outstanding credit include:

- Limits on access to appropriate amounts of financing, with incentives to contain excessively long and heavy use;
- Conditionality and program design;
- Safeguards assessments of central banks;
- Post-program monitoring;
- Measures to deal with misreporting; and
- Voluntary services and supplementary information provided by the IMF, including technical assistance; the transparency initiative, comprising the establishment and monitoring of codes and standards, including statistical standards and codes for monetary and fiscal transparency and the assessment of financial sector soundness; and the improved governance initiative.

Given the monetary character of the IMF and the need for its resources to revolve, members with financial obligations to the institution must repay them as they fall due so that these resources can be made available to other members. Since the early 1980s, the overdue obligations that have emerged have been a matter of concern because they weaken the IMF's liquidity position and impose a cost on other members.

Safeguards put in place to deal with overdue obligations to the IMF include the following two broad areas:

- Policies to assist members in clearing arrears to the IMF, including:

  —the cooperative strategy, consisting of three components: prevention of arrears, collaboration in clearing arrears, and remedial measures, which are intended to have a deterrent effect, for countries that do not cooperate actively; and

— the rights approach, which allows a member in arrears to accumulate "rights" to future disbursements from the IMF.

• Measures to protect the IMF's financial position.

Financial Reporting and Audit Requirements

The IMF's By-Laws mandate that its accounts and statements provide a "true and fair view" of its financial position. The IMF prepares its financial statements in accordance with International Accounting Standards (IAS) but is not bound by specific legal provisions or accounting pronouncements in effect in individual member countries. The IMF is required to publish an *Annual Report* containing audited statements of its accounts and to issue summary statements of its holdings of SDRs, gold, and members' currencies at intervals of three months or less. As part of its financial reporting, the IMF makes extensive information on financial and other activities available to the public on its website (http://www.imf.org) in order to provide a timely and comprehensive view of the IMF's financial position. The IMF's financial year covers the period from May 1 through April 30.

The IMF's finances are analogous to those of other financial institutions, and comparison between the IMF and such institutions has been made easier by recent changes in the presentation of the IMF's financial statements. A typical financial institution holds liquid assets and loan claims and securities among its assets, financed by its deposit (monetary) liabilities and capital resources. Similarly, in the GRA the IMF holds assets (currencies, SDRs, and gold) and credit outstanding to its members, and issues monetary liabilities (referred to as reserve tranche positions), while its capital includes members' quota subscriptions. Similar practices are followed in the financial statements of the SDR Department and of the PRGF and PRGF-HIPC Trusts in order to make their financial operations transparent.

The audit procedures in place call for an external audit of the IMF's accounts and activities. The external audit of the financial statements of the IMF's General Department, SDR Department, Administered Accounts, and Staff Retirement Plans is conducted annually by an external audit firm selected by the Executive Board. The external audit is conducted in accordance with International Standards on Auditing (ISA) under the general oversight of an External Audit Committee (EAC). The EAC consists of three persons, each representing a different member country, who are selected by the Executive Board for an initial term of three years (EAC members may be reappointed for an additional three-year period). The Executive Board approves the terms of reference of the EAC, but the EAC may recommend changes to the terms of reference for the approval of the Executive Board. At least one person on the EAC must be selected from one of the six largest quota holders of the IMF. The nominees must possess the qualifications required to carry out the oversight of the IMF's annual audit and the nominees are therefore typically experienced independent auditors or auditors in public service. The EAC elects one of its members as chairman, determines its own procedures, and is otherwise independent of the management of the IMF in overseeing the annual audit. The audit committee is responsible for transmitting the audit reports issued by the external audit firm to the Board of Governors through the IMF's Managing Director and the Executive Board. The chairman of the EAC is also required to brief the Executive Board on the work of the EAC at the conclusion of the annual audit.

Sources of Information on IMF Finances

IMF's Website

Comprehensive and timely data on IMF finances are available on the IMF website. Through a specially designed portal entitled "IMF Finances" (see http://www.imf.org/external/fin.htm) (Box I.3), which is prominently referenced on the homepage of the IMF website (http://www.imf.org), anyone with access to the Internet can obtain current and historical data on all aspects of IMF lending and borrowing operations. Financial data are updated on a daily, weekly, monthly, or quarterly basis, as appropriate. In addition, the "IMF Finances" portal provides a gateway to a wealth of general information on the financial structure, terms, and operations of the institution, including this pamphlet. The financial data are presented in aggregate form for the institution as a whole, and in country-specific form for each member of the IMF on:

- exchange rates (twice daily)
- IMF interest rates (weekly)
- financial activities and status of lending arrangements (weekly)
- financial resources and liquidity (monthly)

BOX I.3. IMF FINANCES WEBSITE
(HTTP://WWW.IMF.ORG/EXTERNAL/FIN.HTM)

IMF Home | Search | Site Map | Site Index | Help | What's New

International Monetary Fund

About the IMF | News | Publications | Country Info | IMF Finances | Standards & Codes

IMF Finances

Tuesday,
Jul. 31 2001

SDR1 = USD 1.25874
USD1 = SDR 0.794447

Exchange Rates in Terms of SDRs
Current Rates
Current Month

Exchange Rates for
Selected Currencies
Updated at approximately 1:00 PM and 4:00 PM U.S. EST, Monday to Friday

Data Archive
2001, 2000, 1999, 1998, 1997, 1996, 1995

SDR Valuation

The IMF posts SDR rates Monday to Friday except for these holidays

Disclaimer

General Information

Financial Organization & Operations

Quotas, Governors, & Voting Power

Glossary of Financial Terms

Special Drawing Rights (SDRs)

User's Guide to the SDR

Financial Data

Financial Activities: Week-at-a-Glance

Financial Resources & Liquidity Monthly

Financial Transactions Quarterly

Member Financial Data
  By Country
  By Topic
  · Disbursements & Repayments
  · Projected Obligations to the IMF
  · IMF Credit Outstanding
  · Lending Arrangements
  · SDR Allocations & Holdings
  · Arrears

IMF Financial Statements Quarterly

Annual Report

Where does the IMF get its Resources?

Financing the Fund's Operations

Quotas & Quota Reviews

Gold in the IMF

Borrowing Arrangements

IMF Lending

How We Lend

Terms of IMF Lending

Review of the IMF Loan Facilities

Financial Assistance for the Poorest Members

Poverty Reduction & Growth Facility (PRGF)

Debt Initiative for Heavily Indebted Poor Countries (HIPC)

Emergency Assistance

IMF Interest Rates

SDR Interest Rate, Rate of Remuneration and Rate of Charge

Rate of Remuneration, Rate of Charge and Burden Sharing Adjustments updated every Monday

IMF Home··Search··Site Map··Site Index··Help··What's New
About the IMF··News··Publications··Country Info··IMF Finances··Standards & Codes

- financial statements (monthly)
- financing of IMF transactions (quarterly)
- financial position of members in the IMF (monthly)
- disbursements and repayments (monthly)
- projected obligations to the IMF (monthly)
- IMF credit outstanding (monthly)
- lending arrangements (monthly)
- SDR allocations and holdings (monthly)
- arrears to the IMF (monthly)

Contacts in the Treasurer's Department

Questions concerning any aspect of the financial structure and operations of the IMF may be directed to the Treasurer's Department staff directly involved in this work by sending an e-mail inquiry to IMFfinances@imf.org. In the Treasurer's Department of the IMF, financial policy and operational work is organized in units along functional lines. Inquiries may be directed to the Treasurer of the IMF or to the appropriate Division Chief at the address below:

> International Monetary Fund
> 700 19th Street, N.W.
> Washington, D.C. 20431
> United States

Chief, Accounts and Financial Reports Division
- Financial statements and related reports
- Policies to safeguard the IMF's financial position
- Accounting treatment of financial transactions

Chief, Financial Planning and Operations Division
- Planning and execution of financial transactions
- Calculation of SDR value and SDR interest rate

Chief, General Resources and SDR Policy Division
- Terms and general conditions of IMF lending
- Financial resources and liquidity
- Determination of quotas
- Functioning of the SDR system

Chief, PRGF and HIPC Financing Division
- Financing for Poverty Reduction and Growth Facility
- Participation in the Heavily Indebted Poor Countries Initiative
- Arrears to the IMF
- Investment of resources for concessional assistance

Chief, Safeguards Assessment Unit
- Safeguards assessments of central banks of borrowing members

II

General Department

Introduction

The IMF's resources are held in the General Department, which consists of three separate accounts: the General Resources Account (GRA), the Special Disbursement Account (SDA), and the Investment Account.

General Resources Account

The GRA is the principal account of the IMF and handles by far the largest share of transactions between the IMF and its membership. The GRA can best be described as a pool of currencies and reserve assets built up from members' fully paid capital subscriptions in the form of quotas.[1] Quotas are the basic building blocks of the IMF. They broadly reflect each member's relative economic size, taking into account the quotas of similar countries. Quotas determine the maximum amount of financial resources that a member is obligated to provide to the IMF, voting power in IMF decision making, and a member's share of SDR allocations. The financial assistance a member may obtain from the IMF is also generally based on its quota.

The financial structure of the IMF rests on the principle that quota subscriptions are the basic source of financing for the GRA. A quarter of a member's quota subscription is normally paid in reserve assets, with the remainder paid in the member's own currency.[2] Currencies held by the IMF are of two types, usable and unusable. A currency is usable if the issuing member's external payments position is strong enough for it to be called upon to finance IMF credit to other members. Other currencies, that is, the

---

[1]Reserve assets are those that are readily available and accepted for international payments, such as the four currencies currently recognized as "freely usable" by the IMF: the U.S. dollar, euro, Japanese yen, and pound sterling. A freely usable currency is one that the IMF determines is widely used to make payments for international transactions and is traded in the principal exchange markets.

[2]Prior to the Second Amendment of the IMF Articles on April 1, 1978, the reserve asset portion was paid in gold, and after that, in SDRs or "usable" currencies of other members as determined by the IMF.

currencies of borrowers or financially weak members, are considered unusable. Thus, a portion of the GRA's pool of resources consists of currencies that cannot be used, leaving the IMF's effective lending capacity at about half of total quotas.[3]

The IMF may also supplement its quota resources by borrowing and through additions to its precautionary balances. These balances comprise reserves in the GRA as well as resources that have been set aside in the first Special Contingent Account (SCA-1) to protect against the risk of overdue payments. These resources are not segregated from other resources of the GRA and can therefore finance the extension of credit.

With its usable resources, the IMF provides financing to its member countries. Members "borrow" from the GRA under the IMF's "credit tranche" policies or under special policies or facilities.[4] The credit tranches provide financing for balance of payments need, arising from almost any cause, whereas credits under other facilities deal with needs arising from specified causes. Financial assistance is typically made available in installments that are linked to the borrowing country's observance of specific economic and financial policy conditions that must be met before the next installment is released. These conditions are agreed with the member under agreements called "arrangements." Members using IMF resources pay a market-based rate of interest on their outstanding use of credit from the IMF.

A member's financial position in the IMF is measured by the GRA's holdings of its currency relative to quota. Members draw on the IMF's pool of members' currencies and SDRs through a purchase-repurchase mechanism (Box II.1). A member obtaining resources from the IMF "purchases" either SDRs or the currency of another member in exchange for an equivalent amount (in SDR terms) of its own currency, and later reverses the transaction

---

[3]A member with usable currency pays in a usable currency whereas other members pay only the reserve asset portion in usable currency. Any member may pay the reserve asset portion in SDRs. Currencies are held by the IMF in depository accounts at members' central banks. Payment of the nonreserve asset portion of quota subscriptions is normally in the form of promissory notes (nonnegotiable, non-interest-bearing securities) that are converted into currency on demand.

[4]GRA credit is normally governed by the IMF's general lending policies (also known as "credit tranche" policies), as opposed to the special policies that apply to other types of credit. Both sets of policies are discussed in the section "Credit Outstanding." IMF credit has traditionally been provided in "tranches" (segments), equivalent to 25 percent of quota, as explained in the section "Credit Tranche Policies." "Borrowing" is undertaken through the purchase-repurchase mechanism, which is discussed in Box II.1.

BOX II.1. THE IMF'S MAJOR FINANCING MECHANISM

The IMF's lending is financed from the capital subscribed by member countries. Each country is assigned a quota that determines its maximum financial commitment to the IMF. A portion of the quota is provided in the form of reserve assets (foreign currencies acceptable to the IMF or SDRs) and the remainder in its own currency. The IMF extends financing by providing reserve assets to the borrower from the reserve asset subscriptions of members or by calling on countries that are considered financially strong to exchange their currency subscriptions for reserve assets.

The loan is disbursed or drawn by the borrower "purchasing" the reserve assets from the IMF with its own currency.[1] Repayment of the loan is achieved by the borrower "repurchasing" its currency from the IMF with reserve assets. The IMF levies a basic rate of interest (charges) on loans based on the SDR interest rate and imposes surcharges depending on the amount and maturity of the loan and the level of credit outstanding.

A country that provides reserve assets to the IMF as part of its quota subscription or through the use of its currency receives a liquid claim on the IMF (a reserve, or reserve tranche, position) which can be encashed on demand to obtain reserve assets to meet a balance of payments financing need.

These claims earn interest (remuneration) based on the SDR interest rate and are considered by members as part of their international reserve assets. As IMF loans are repaid (repurchased) by the borrower with reserve assets, these funds are transferred to the creditor countries in exchange for their currencies and the creditor claim on the IMF is extinguished.

The purchase-repurchase approach to IMF lending affects the composition of the IMF's resources but not the overall size. An increase in loans outstanding will reduce the IMF's holdings of reserve assets and the currencies of members that are financially strong and increase the IMF's holdings of the currencies of countries that are borrowing from the IMF. The amount of the IMF's holdings of reserve assets and the currencies of financially strong countries determines the IMF's lending capacity (liquidity).

While the purchase-repurchase mechanism is not technically or legally a "loan," it is the functional equivalent of a loan. Similarly, IMF lending "arrangements" provide for drawings in installments upon the fulfillment of certain policy conditions. Thus, they are similar to conditional lines of credit. For ease of reference, these more commonly understood terms are often used in this pamphlet rather than the unique internal IMF terminology.

---

[1]In making a purchase, the member provides domestic currency to the IMF additional to currency previously paid to the IMF for the member's quota subscription.

by a "repurchase" of its currency held by the IMF with SDRs or the currency of another member.[5]

Members receive a liquid claim on the IMF (called a reserve, or reserve tranche, position) for the reserve assets they provide to the IMF. This claim earns a market-related rate of interest (called remuneration) and can be encashed on demand to obtain reserve assets from the IMF. Consequently, a member's provision of reserve assets to the IMF changes the composition of the member's reserve assets—from, for example, U.S. dollars to claims on the IMF—rather than the overall size of its international reserve assets. As the borrower repays the IMF loan (repurchases its currency with reserve assets), these funds are transferred to the creditor countries in exchange for their currencies, and the creditor's claim on the IMF is extinguished.

A member's purchase of currency reduces the IMF's holdings of the currency purchased, enlarges the reserve tranche position of the country whose currency is purchased, and increases the IMF's holdings of the purchasing member's currency. Charges (interest) are not levied on purchases within the reserve tranche, as these resources are the member's own reserves. Interest is charged on the use of IMF credit, which is obtained through purchases outside of the reserve tranche. A member can choose whether or not to use its reserve tranche before utilizing IMF credit. Alternative financial positions of members in the IMF's pool of resources in the GRA are illustrated in Figure II.1.

The currency purchased from the IMF must be that of a member with a strong external position, whose subscribed currency is considered usable for IMF transactions. If the currency purchased is not freely usable, the member whose currency is purchased is obliged to exchange purchased amounts of its currency for freely usable currencies. If the purchased currency is freely usable, the borrower can undertake transactions in the private exchange markets or with the issuer of the freely usable currency to acquire a different currency. A member whose currency is being used is obligated, if necessary, to provide an amount of reserve assets of up to 100 percent of its quota. The amount of reserve assets provided to the IMF has in practice fallen well short of this maximum. In planning and executing members' transactions, members' currencies are used in the financing of IMF credit according to their relative quota shares. In turn, members' currencies are used in effect-

---

[5]This financing mechanism has its roots in the credit facilities that existed between central banks before the IMF was established.

Figure II.1. Member Financial Positions in the GRA

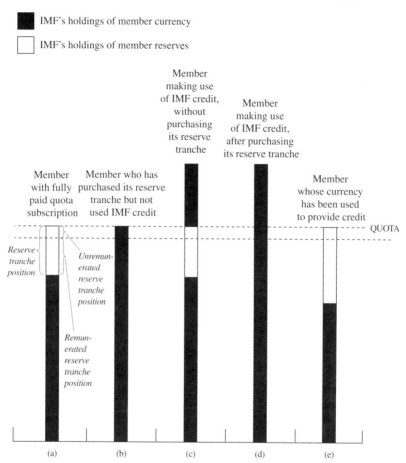

Situation (a): A member has paid its quota subscription in full and not drawn on its reserve tranche. The remunerated reserve tranche position excludes certain holdings (holdings acquired as a result of a member's use of IMF credit and holdings in the IMF No. 2 Account that are less than $\frac{1}{10}$ of 1 percent of quota; see "IMF Accounts in Member Countries"). See text for an explanation of the unremunerated portion of the reserve tranche.

Situation (b): The member has drawn its reserve tranche in full. The reserve tranche purchase is not subject to charges (interest).

Situation (c): The member is using IMF resources but has not drawn its reserve tranche. The level of holdings in excess of the member's quota is subject to charges.

Situation (d): The member is using IMF resources, in addition to having drawn its reserve tranche. The level of holdings in excess of the member's quota is subject to charges.

Situation (e): The IMF has made use of the member's currency and pays the member remuneration on its enlarged reserve tranche position.

23

ing receipts to the IMF in a manner that adjusts reserve tranche positions toward a uniform proportion of their quotas.[6]

The purchase-repurchase mechanism explains why, from an accounting perspective, the IMF's total resources do not vary as a result of the IMF's financial assistance—only the composition of its assets change. Moreover, the value of members' currencies held in the GRA's pool of resources is maintained in SDR terms over time through periodic additions to the amounts of currencies that are depreciating against the SDR and reductions from those that are appreciating against the SDR. This maintenance of value provision is an obligation of members under the Articles.[7]

Special Disbursement Account

The Special Disbursement Account (SDA) is the vehicle for receiving and investing profits from the sale of the IMF's gold (i.e., the net proceeds in excess of the book value of SDR 35 a fine ounce), and for making transfers to other accounts for special purposes authorized in the Articles, in particular for financial assistance to low-income members of the IMF.

Investment Account

The IMF is authorized to establish an Investment Account in the General Department; to date, however, no decision has been taken to this effect. Investments of amounts up to the level of accumulated reserves may be made only in income-generating marketable obligations of international financial organizations or of the member whose currency is used for the investment.[8] The income may be reinvested or used to meet the expenses of conducting the business of the IMF, including both operational and administrative expenses.

---

[6]For an analysis of the key elements underlying the GRA's costs and revenues and past proposals for simplification or modification, see "Financing the Fund's Operations—Review of Issues," March 2000, on the IMF's website (http://www.imf.org/external/np/tre/ffo/2001/fin.htm).

[7]Article V, Section 11(a).

[8]The resources in the GRA are managed in such a way as to lower the IMF's costs or to increase the IMF's revenue. In order to be more profitable than GRA resources, resources in an Investment Account would need to be invested at a rate that exceeds the SDR interest rate after taking into account any exchange risk.

The Balance Sheet

The relationships among the sources and uses of resources in the General Department, and their relative magnitudes, are summarized in its balance sheet (Table II.1).

On the asset side, the first major item is credit outstanding at the end of FY2001 of SDR 42.2 billion, which is the value of financing extended by the IMF to its members. Financing to debtor members is largely funded by the use of the currencies of creditor members and is reflected in the resulting reserve tranche positions of creditor members (see Box II.1). Members with outstanding credit pay a market-related rate of interest on these loans which fully covers the payment of interest to the creditors providing the resources to the IMF, as further explained below. The vast bulk of other assets held by the IMF in the GRA was usable and other currencies, equal to SDR 165.7 billion. Gold, valued at SDR 5.9 billion, represented a relatively small share of total assets.[9] The IMF receives no interest on its gold or currency holdings that do not result from the extension of IMF credit. The only interest-bearing asset held by the IMF other than its outstanding credit is its holdings of SDRs, which were SDR 2.4 billion. With the addition of some minor receivables and other assets, total assets of the GRA at end-April 2001 amounted to SDR 217.5 billion.

On the resources and liabilities side, total quota resources were SDR 212.4 billion on April 30, 2001. As noted above, some of these subscription resources were usable and some were not. Usable currencies amounted to SDR 109.7 billion and unusable currencies SDR 56.0 billion. In addition, there were SDR 46.7 billion in reserve tranche positions of members. The reserve tranche positions of IMF members result from initial quota payments and the increase due to the extension of IMF credit to other members. These reserve positions earn a market-related rate of return, as explained below. Precautionary balances, which include reserves and the balance in the Special Contingent Account (SCA), amounted to an additional SDR 4.5 billion. Adding a small amount of interest (remuneration) payable and some other minor liabilities gives a total of SDR 217.5 billion of GRA resources and liabilities.

---

[9]The IMF's holdings of gold are valued at historical cost. For most of the gold holdings, this is SDR 35 a fine ounce. Market prices for gold are much higher, which imparts a fundamental strength to the IMF's financial position. See the discussion below in the section on "Gold Holdings."

TABLE II.1. BALANCE SHEET OF THE GENERAL DEPARTMENT,
AS OF APRIL 30, 2001
(In billions of SDRs)

Assets		Resources and Liabilities	
General Resources Account:		*General Resources Account:*	
		Members' resources:	
		Quota subscriptions, represented by:	
Credit outstanding	42.2	Reserve tranche positions	46.7
Usable currencies	109.7	Usable currencies	109.7
Other currencies	56.0	Other currencies	56.0
Total currencies	207.9	Total quotas	212.4
		Precautionary balances:	
		Reserves of the GRA	3.3
		SCA-1	1.2
			4.5
SDR holdings	2.4	Liabilities:	
Gold holdings	5.9	Remuneration payable	0.4
Receivables	0.6	Other liabilities	0.2
Other assets	0.7	Total liabilities	0.6
Total GRA	217.5	Total GRA	217.5
Special Disbursement Account:		*Special Disbursement Account:*	
Investments of the SDA	2.4	Accumulated resources of the SDA	2.8
SAF loans	0.4		
Total SDA	2.8		
Total assets	220.3	Total resources and liabilities	220.3

Note: Numbers may not add to totals due to rounding.

At end-April 2001, the IMF did not have any outstanding borrowing, but if it had, the amount of borrowing outstanding would have been shown on the liabilities side, with additional offsetting credit extended by the IMF to its members on the asset side. A comparison of the relative size of these resources and liabilities demonstrates that the IMF is overwhelmingly a quota-based institution.

26

The rest of the General Department consists solely of the relatively small amount of assets and liabilities of the SDA, SDR 2.8 billion at end-April 2001. These represent the accumulated resources of the account, which reflect the profits and investment returns realized on past gold sales on the resources side, and the investment of these resources on the asset side. The income from these investments is transferred to the PRGF and PRGF-HIPC Trusts to provide concessional financial assistance to low-income members. There was also a small amount (SDR 0.4 billion) of loans still outstanding from the Structural Adjustment Facility (SAF) at end-April 2001.[10] These loans were financed with SDA resources.

The remainder of this chapter expands upon the above discussion. It first discusses each item on the asset side of the GRA — namely, credit outstanding, which includes a description of the various terms and conditions of IMF lending, followed by relatively short sections on currency, SDR, and gold holdings. It then describes each item on the resources and liabilities side of the GRA — namely, quotas, including reserve tranche positions, and precautionary balances. Next, the chapter explains how the supply of and demand for GRA resources is managed through the quarterly financial transactions plan, and how the IMF monitors its overall level of liquidity in the GRA. Finally, it shows how IMF transactions are reflected in the accounts and balance sheets of member countries.

The management and investment strategy for the resources in the SDA is covered in Chapter IV.

The Asset Side

Credit Outstanding

Credit outstanding, as the caption suggests, represents loans already provided to members under the various IMF facilities. This section first describes the general terms and conditions of IMF lending, followed by a discussion of the IMF's financial policies and lending facilities.

---

[10]The SAF is discussed in Chapter IV.

General Terms and Conditions

Balance of Payments Need

Members using IMF resources must have a balance of payments need. A borrowing member cannot use IMF resources in the absence of a representation of balance of payments need, and the extent of their use cannot exceed that need. Borrowing usually takes place under an IMF arrangement, which is similar to a conditional line of credit and is associated with the implementation of an economic reform program in a member country. The most common type of arrangement is a Stand-By Arrangement in the credit tranches or an arrangement under the Extended Fund Facility (EFF).[11] Such arrangements can be approved on the basis of a prospective balance of payments need, although the existence of a balance of payments need does not, in itself, entitle a member to draw on the IMF.

The concept of balance of payments need has evolved over time. The concept includes three distinct elements: the balance of payments position of the member, its foreign reserve position, and developments in its reserve position.[12] These three elements are regarded as separate, and a representation of need can be based on any one of them. An operational framework has been developed over the years to serve as the basis for judgments on the magnitude of balance of payments deficits and the adequacy of foreign reserves. In the implementation of this framework, the circumstances of members are taken into account.

Once an arrangement has been approved by the IMF, a member's representation of balance of payments need to make a purchase is not subject to challenge, under a long-standing policy intended to assure the member of the availability of IMF resources committed to it, subject only to its meeting conditions specified in the arrangement. However, the IMF may take remedial action after a purchase under an arrangement or a reserve tranche purchase if it finds that the conditions for the purchase were not met, including that of balance of payments need.

Other conditions may also be required. The IMF's policies under particular facilities may also stipulate requirements concerning the origins and nature of the underlying balance of payments disequilibrium. For instance,

---

[11]See discussion below under "Financial Policies and Facilities."

[12]Article V, Section 3(b)(ii).

the use of the Compensatory Financing Facility (CFF) is restricted to temporary balance of payments deficits arising from overall export shortfalls or increased costs of specified cereal imports.

Access Policy

The policy of the IMF is to encourage members to approach it for assistance at an early stage of their balance of payments difficulties. Members experiencing balance of payments problems can approach the IMF, but are under no obligation to do so at any time. Over the years, it has come to be recognized that the efficacy of the mixture of adjustment polices and financing depends largely on the early adoption of corrective policy measures. Early resort to an adjustment program supported by IMF resources can help to avoid more drastic policy actions that may otherwise be required, thereby limiting the impact of the adjustment on other members.

Quantitative limits on access are used to ensure equal treatment of members. Access limits are set in terms of quota, the basic measure of members' financial rights and obligations in the IMF. For the credit tranches and the EFF, which account for the lion's share of IMF lending, the current limits take the form of an annual limit of 100 percent of quota on purchases over any 12-month period and a cumulative limit of 300 percent of quota on the level of IMF credit outstanding. Average annual access under these lending arrangements in recent years has been 40–50 percent of quota (Figure II.2). Other IMF facilities are subject to separate access limits or, in some cases, no explicit limits (Box II.2). In exceptional circumstances, these limits can be waived, as they were for members most immediately affected by the severe financial crises of the late 1990s.

The level of access to GRA resources under Stand-By Arrangements and the EFF — that is, the amount that can be borrowed — is based on criteria that are applied uniformly to all members. These criteria seek to balance the needs of members against the overarching responsibility of the institution to safeguard and ensure the temporary use of its resources. The criteria are:

- actual or potential need for resources from the IMF, taking into account other sources of financing and the desirability of maintaining a reasonable level of reserves;
- ability to service indebtedness to the IMF, thereby protecting the revolving character of IMF resources;
- amount of the outstanding use of IMF credit and record in using IMF resures in the past.

FIGURE II.2. AVERAGE ANNUAL ACCESS UNDER STAND-BY AND EXTENDED ARRANGEMENTS[1]

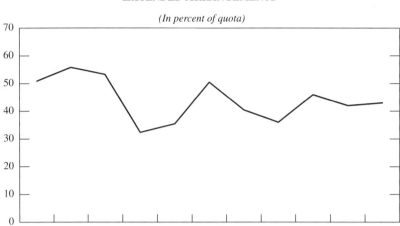

(In percent of quota)

[1]Excluding the cases with exceptional access (i.e., exceeding the access limits). Excluded arrangements are Mexico's 1995 Stand-By Arrangement; Indonesia's, Korea's and Thailand's 1997 Stand-By Arrangements; Brazil's 1998 Stand-By Arrangement; Indonesia's 1998 Extended Arrangement; Turkey's 1999 Stand-By Arrangement; and Indonesia's 2000 Extended Arrangement.

Phasing of Purchases

An important feature of IMF lending is the phasing of disbursements. All arrangements above 25 percent of quota in the credit tranches—the upper credit tranches—and under the EFF are subject to conditionality and the phasing of purchases (see Chapter V). Purchases in the first credit tranche (up to 25 percent of quota) are not phased, but do incorporate some policy conditionality.

Phasing refers to the practice of making IMF resources available in installments over the period of an arrangement, typically quarterly, subject to the observance of performance criteria, the completion of a program review, or both.[13] This is intended to ensure that IMF financing goes hand in hand with

---

[13]An "arrangement" is an assurance by the IMF that it stands ready to provide foreign exchange or SDRs under certain conditions during a specified period of time. The arrangement is in support of a detailed economic "adjustment program" of the member. See the Glossary for definitions of these terms.

BOX II.2. THE FRAMEWORK FOR ACCESS TO IMF RESOURCES

Quota-based access limits

• The *credit tranches* (mainly accessed through Stand-By Arrangements) and the *Extended Fund Facility* (EFF) are subject to the same access limits. These consist of an annual limit of 100 percent of quota and a cumulative limit of 300 percent of quota. The annual limit applies to gross purchases in any 12-month period. The cumulative limit applies to credit outstanding, less scheduled repurchases, plus scheduled purchases, over the period of commitment of resources. These limits may be exceeded in exceptional circumstances. Average annual access has been fairly stable at around half of the annual limit in recent years (see Figure II.2).

• Access under the *Compensatory Financing Facility* (CFF) is subject to its own limits. These limits are cumulative, and include limits of 45 percent of quota each for access under the export shortfalls and excess cereal imports elements, and a combined limit of 55 percent of quota. These limits cannot be exceeded.

• The amount of *emergency assistance* for natural disasters and for post-conflict cases is limited, in any one instance, to 25 percent of quota. Larger amounts can be made available on an exceptional basis in post-conflict cases. Emergency assistance was until recently subject to the access limits under the credit tranches but was converted into a facility and excluded from these access limits, pending further review.

Access to other facilities

• The *Supplemental Reserve Facility* (SRF) is not subject to explicit access limits. SRF resources are provided under Stand-By or Extended Arrangements in addition to credit tranche or EFF resources, which are subject to annual and cumulative limits. The IMF uses the same criteria for access to its resources under all policies and facilities (see section on "General Terms and Conditions") but in the case of the SRF also takes into account the liquidity position of the IMF, given the magnitude of the balance of payments need in cases qualifying for this facility.

• The *Contingent Credit Lines* (CCLs) are not subject to access limits but commitments under the CCL are expected to be in the range of 300–500 percent of quota. CCL resources are provided under Stand-By Arrangements, in combination with credit tranche resources up to the annual or the cumulative limit. As with the SRF, the liquidity position of the IMF is taken into account when determining access under the CCL.

---

policy measures that are considered necessary to resolve underlying balance of payments problems and enable members to repay the IMF within the established repurchase period. Phasing also enables the purchasing member to demonstrate to other members that its adjustment program is being implemented and warrants their continued support.

The choice between even phasing and uneven phasing depends on the balance of payments need and the path of adjustment. These choices are made on a case-by-case basis: resources are normally fairly evenly spread over the arrangement period but a concentration of adjustment at the beginning of an arrangement could justify front-loading of purchases. The frequency of purchases may also be affected by the length of lags in the reporting of data relating to performance criteria.[14]

Repurchase Policies

The repurchase policies of the IMF are intended to ensure the revolving character of its resources. All purchases made from the IMF are subject to predetermined repurchase schedules (Table II.2). The length of the repurchase period and the number of repurchase installments differ according to the policy or facility under which the credit was extended.

In the case of most purchases, a borrower is expected to repurchase earlier than the schedule of repurchase obligations. Such time-based repurchase expectations are aimed at securing early repayment from members in a position to do so, in keeping with a long-standing principle of the IMF that its resources should be used only as long as there is a balance of payments need (Box II.3). A waiver of early repurchase expectations can be provided by the Executive Board upon the request of a member, if the member's external position is not strong enough for the member to pay early without undue hardship or risk. In case of a waiver, repurchases would fall due according to the original obligation schedule.

Time-based repurchase expectations apply to purchases made after November 28, 2000 in the credit tranches and under the CFF and EFF. For purchases in the credit tranches and under the CFF, the expectation schedule is 1 year in advance of the obligation schedule, beginning 2¼ years after each purchase and ending after 4 years. For the EFF, the expectation schedule

---

[14]Specific guidelines on phasing are set out in *Selected Decisions and Selected Documents of the International Monetary Fund* (Washington). This volume is updated annually on June 30. See, for example, the Twenty-Fifth Issue, June 30, 2000.

TABLE II.2. FINANCIAL TERMS OF IMF CREDIT

Instrument	Charges				Repurchases		
	Base	Surcharge	Service	Commitment	Expectation	Obligation	Installments
First credit tranche	Basic rate	100 basis points for credit over 200 percent of quota; 200 basis points for credit over 300 percent of quota	50 basis points	None	2¼–4 years	3¼–5 years	8 quarterly
Stand-By Arrangement	Basic rate		50 basis points		2¼–4 years	3¼–5 years	8 quarterly
Extended Fund Facility (EFF)	Basic rate		50 basis points		4½–7 years	4½–10 years	6 semiannual / 12 semiannual
Supplemental Reserve Facility (SRF)	Basic rate	300–500 basis points initial surcharge rises by 50 basis points after one year and each subsequent six months	50 basis points	25 basis points plus 10 basis points for amounts in excess of 100% of quota	1–1½ years	2–2½ years	2 semiannual
Contingent Credit Line (CCL)	Basic rate	150–350 basis points	50 basis points		1–1½ years	2–2½ years	2 semiannual
Compensatory Financing Facility (CFF)	Basic rate	None	50 basis points	None	2¼–4 years	3¼–5 years	8 quarterly
Emergency assistance	Basic rate	None	50 basis points	None	None	3¼–5 years	8 quarterly

The *basic rate of charge* is linked directly to the SDR interest rate by a coefficient that is fixed each financial year. The basic rate of charge therefore fluctuates with the market rate for the SDR, which is calculated on a weekly basis. The basic rate of charge is adjusted upward for burden sharing to compensate for the overdue charges of other members (see Box II.9). The *surcharge* on high levels of credit outstanding under the credit tranches and the EFF is designed to discourage large use of IMF resources. The *SRF and CCL surcharges* increase with the time elapsed since the first SRF or CCL purchase, which sharpens the incentive for repurchases ahead of the obligation schedule. The annual *commitment fee* applies to amounts available under an arrangement during the year. The fee is refunded to the extent that available amounts are purchased.

Repurchases are made in equal installments at regular intervals over a fixed period. A member is free to repurchase in advance of maturity and to attribute repurchases to any outstanding obligation to the IMF. The repurchase obligation schedule for each type of credit is generally associated with an accelerated schedule, which members are expected to follow. A member not in a position to meet the expectations schedule can request an extension up to the corresponding period in the obligation schedule.

BOX II.3. EVOLUTION OF IMF POLICIES ON REPURCHASES

Under the original Articles of Agreement, there were no fixed repurchase periods for the use of IMF resources: repurchases were calculated annually for each member according to a formula based on their international reserves. This reflected the principle that the IMF's resources are made available only to members with a balance of payments and reserve need, and was designed to ensure their revolving character.

This approach became unworkable over time, however, and was increasingly supplemented by policies on repurchase periods. The coexistence of these two approaches—one based on explicit schedules and another on reserve strength—was codified under the Second Amendment of the Articles in 1978 with the establishment of fixed repurchase periods (Article V, Section 7(c)) and provision for early repurchase by members as their balance of payments and reserve position improves (Article V, Section 7(b)).

A major change in the repurchase policies was introduced in 1997 with the establishment of the SRF to help members experiencing exceptional balance of payments difficulties owing to a large short-term financing need resulting from a sudden and disruptive loss of market confidence. In line with the short-term nature of this type of balance of payments need, the SRF incorporates much shorter repurchase periods and features repurchase expectations that are legally outside of the framework of Article V, Section 7(b). Repurchases under the SRF are expected to be made in two installments after 1 and 1½ years from the date of the purchase. In order to provide flexibility for cases where the member's return to capital markets takes longer than anticipated, each repurchase can be extended by up to 1 year, upon request by the member and approval of the request by the Executive Board. The same repurchase profile was adopted for the CCL in 1999.

Repurchase expectations were introduced for purchases in the credit tranches and under the EFF and the CFF in November 2000. These time-based repurchase expectations (see Table II.2) can be extended upon request by the member, in which case repurchases would fall due according to the original obligation schedule. Waivers are considered by the Executive Board if the member's external position is not strong enough for the member to pay early without undue hardship or risk. Adjustment programs supported by credit tranche or EFF resources are generally designed on the basis of the obligation schedule for repurchases, so that in most cases members will be in a position to meet repurchase expectations only if their external position is stronger than projected at the outset of the program. In contrast, adjustment programs supported by SRF and CCL resources are designed on the basis of the expectation schedule from repurchases.

---

begins after 4½ years, as with the obligation schedule, but repurchases are doubled, so that the expectation schedule ends after 7 years rather than 10 years under the obligation schedule. Figure II.3 illustrates the mapping of repurchase expectations and the corresponding repurchase obligations.

A member can request an extension of time-based repurchase expectations if its external position is not sufficiently strong. If the IMF agrees to an extension, all repurchase expectations during the period covered by the extension would revert back to the corresponding repurchase obligations. There is a presumption that this period would be one year, although a longer or shorter period could be set. If the IMF does not agree to an extension, the member would be expected to make repurchases according to the expectation schedule. Failure to do so would result in a suspension of the right to make further purchases, including prospective purchases under an existing arrangement. However, the member would not be in arrears until it failed to meet a repurchase obligation.

IMF-supported programs are guided by the requirement that the member should be able to meet repurchase obligations. In most cases, therefore, members will be considered to be in a position to meet repurchase expectations only if their external position is stronger than had been projected at the time of approval of the associated IMF arrangement. Similarly, the evaluation of members' capacity to repay the IMF is based on the obligation schedule.

An early repurchase policy serves as a backstop to the standard repurchase provisions. Members with IMF credit outstanding are normally expected to make repurchases as their balance of payments and reserve position improves.[15] A member could experience an especially rapid and strong turnaround in its balance of payments and reserve position, and may be in a position to make repurchases earlier than under the fixed schedules for time-based repurchase expectations. In addition, there are some purchases for which time-based repurchase expectations are not applicable.[16] Judgments on the appropriateness of early repurchases in individual cases are made by the Executive Board. The amount of such repurchases expected during a given quarter is determined on the basis of a formula that relies heavily on gross reserves (Box II.4).

---

[15]Article V, Section 7(b).

[16]Time-based repurchase expectations do not apply to purchases made prior to November 2000 or to purchases under emergency assistance; separate repurchase expectations apply to purchases under the CCL and SRF.

FIGURE II.3. EARLY REPURCHASE EXPECTATIONS

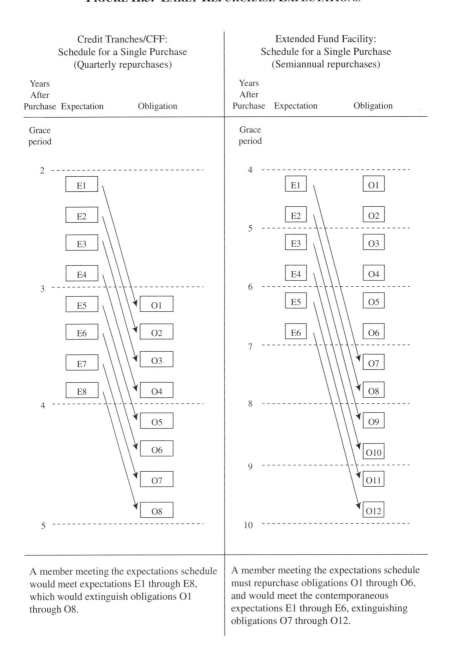

A member meeting the expectations schedule would meet expectations E1 through E8, which would extinguish obligations O1 through O8.

A member meeting the expectations schedule must repurchase obligations O1 through O6, and would meet the contemporaneous expectations E1 through E6, extinguishing obligations O7 through O12.

BOX II.4. EARLY REPURCHASE POLICY: MINIMUM REPURCHASE AMOUNTS

Formula

Under the guidelines for early repurchase, the minimum amount that a member is expected to repurchase each quarter is determined by a formula based on the member's gross international reserves:

- 1.5 percent of latest reserves plus (minus)
- 5.0 percent of the increase (decrease) in reserves over the previous six months.

For this purpose, the IMF uses the latest data on the member's gross reserves as reported in the IMF's *International Financial Statistics*, with gold valued at SDR 35 an ounce, available when the associated financial transactions plan is prepared for Executive Board consideration. The formula thus ensures a tight link between reserves and repayments to the IMF, with any increase in reserves resulting in larger repurchases and vice versa. The formula is applied anew for every quarter the member is included in the transactions plan for early repurchases.

Limits

The minimum repurchase amount is subject to quantitative limits. This amount cannot

- exceed 4 percent of latest reserves in a quarter,
- exceed 10 percent of latest reserves in a year, or
- reduce latest reserves below 250 percent of quota.

These limits are a means to protect members from having to draw too heavily on their owned reserves to meet IMF repayments. In the two decades since the policy was established, early repurchase amounts generated by the formula have always fallen below these limits.

Credits

In addition to these limits, the minimum repurchase amount is reduced to the extent of any repurchase obligations falling due during the quarter or to give credit for voluntary advance repurchases:

- in the two quarters prior to the member being included for early repurchase, or
- subsequent repurchases in excess of minimum repurchase amounts.

The credits are intended to encourage members to accelerate repurchases voluntarily on their own terms.

37

Early repurchase expectations can arise in other contexts. Provisions for early repurchase are built into the CFF, Contingent Credit Line (CCL), and Supplemental Reserve Facility (SRF). In addition, a member is required to take corrective action by making an early repurchase in the event that it makes a purchase under an arrangement that it was not entitled to make by the terms of the arrangement — that is, a noncomplying purchase. The requirement of corrective action can be waived if the IMF decides that the circumstances justify continued use of the purchased resources. A noncomplying purchase would arise if a member were permitted to make a purchase because, on the basis of information available at the time, the IMF was satisfied that the conditions applicable to the purchase under the arrangement had been observed but, on the basis of information subsequently available, it became evident that the conditions of the arrangement had not actually been met.[17]

The IMF can change the period of repurchases.[18] It has the authority to postpone the date for the discharge of a repurchase by a majority of the votes cast, provided that the postponement does not cause the repurchase to exceed the maximum repurchase period. Postponement beyond the maximum period allowed under the arrangement would be considered only in the event that the IMF determined that discharge on the due date would result in exceptional hardship for the member and if the longer period for repurchase is consistent with the revolving nature of the use of IMF resources. Such a decision requires approval by a 70 percent majority of the total voting power.[19]

A member is free to make advance repurchases at any time. At the discretion of the member, advance repurchases can be attributed to any outstanding purchases. In this way, a member is free to reduce the IMF's holdings of its currency corresponding to prior purchases and thereby reduce or eliminate its obligation to pay interest to the IMF. Repurchases can be made, at the choice of the repurchasing member, in SDRs or in currencies selected by the IMF according to the policies and procedures for the use and receipt of

---

[17]See also the discussion in Chapter V on "Measures to Deal with Misreporting."

[18]An 85 percent majority of the total voting power in the IMF is required to change the period of repurchase of holdings of currency acquired by the IMF pursuant to its policy on the use of general resources. A 70 percent majority is required in the case of holdings of currency not acquired as a result of purchases and subject to charges under Article V, Section 8(b)(ii). See Appendix II.

[19]No such decision has been taken in the past 25 years.

currencies under the quarterly financial transactions plan, as discussed below under "Financial Transactions Plan."[20]

Financial Policies and Facilities

The lending instruments of the IMF have evolved over the years. In its early years, IMF lending took place exclusively on the basis of general policies on access in what became known as the credit tranches and, in particular, under Stand-By Arrangements. Beginning in the 1960s, special policies were developed to deal with various balance of payments problems having particular causes, resulting over time in a multiplicity of policies on the use of IMF resources.[21] Special policies on the use of IMF resources outside the credit tranches are generally referred to as facilities.

All decisions on the extension of IMF credit are taken by the Executive Board. These decisions are supported by a formal request from the member and an assessment by the staff of the nature and magnitude of the balance of payments problem, the adequacy of the policy response, and the capacity of the member to repay the IMF. In 1995, the IMF specified streamlined procedures under an Emergency Financing Mechanism to allow for quicker Executive Board approval of IMF financial support. This mechanism is used in circumstances representing, or threatening, a crisis in a member's external accounts that requires an immediate response from the IMF, as was the case in 1997 for Indonesia, Korea, the Philippines, and Thailand and in July 1998 for Russia.

A fundamental review of IMF financial policies and facilities took place in 2000, which resulted in a more streamlined structure, with a sharper focus on crisis prevention and ensuring effective use of IMF resources. This section describes the current structure of policies and facilities; earlier lending instruments are noted in Box II.5.

---

[20]Members have the option of combining all repurchases due within a calendar month, provided that the combined repurchase is completed not later than the last day of the month and that no single repurchase remains outstanding for a period exceeding the maximum permitted under the relevant policy of the IMF.

[21]A comprehensive discussion of the evolution of IMF lending instruments is available on the web: "Review of Facilities—Preliminary Considerations," www.imf.org/external/np/pdr/fac/2000/index.htm.

BOX II.5. EARLIER IMF LENDING INSTRUMENTS

Over the years, the IMF has established a number of policies and facilities to meet particular balance of payments needs that were eventually either eliminated or allowed to lapse:

- The *Buffer Stock Financing Facility*, created in 1969 and eliminated in 2000, provided financing to members to help finance their contributions to approved commodity price stabilization funds.

- The first *Oil Facility* was created in June 1974 in response to the oil price shock, and lapsed in December 1974. A second *Oil Facility* was created in April 1975 to provide additional financing, and lapsed in March 1976.

- A policy of support for *debt and debt-service operations*, initiated in 1989, was a key element of the IMF's response to the debt crisis. The policy proved useful in facilitating commercial bank debt reduction but, by the late 1990s, had outlived its usefulness and was discontinued in 2000.

- An *oil import element* was added to the Compensatory Financing Facility (CFF) in November 1990, when oil prices rose sharply during the Middle East conflict. It was allowed to lapse at end-1991.

- The *Systemic Transformation Facility*, created in April 1993 and allowed to lapse in April 1995, provided support for the early stages of transition from centrally planned to market economies, in relatively small amounts and with relatively low conditionality.

- The policy on *currency stabilization funds* was established in 1995 as a means of providing additional, precautionary support under IMF arrangements during the early stage of an exchange rate–based stabilization program. No member made use of the policy, and it was discontinued in 2000.

- A *contingency element* was added to the CFF in 1988. Until its elimination in 2000, this instrument provided additional access under arrangements, according to prespecified calculations, in the event of unanticipated adverse current account developments.

- The *Y2K Facility* was created in September 1999 to deal with possible strains resulting from the Millennium (Y2K) computer dating problem. It was not used, and lapsed in March 2000.

Credit Tranche Policies

From its early history, IMF credit was made available in tranches (segments). Members could make purchases in four credit tranches, each equivalent to 25 percent of quota, within the prevailing annual access limit of 25 percent of quota and the cumulative access limit of 100 percent of quota. A purchase in the first credit tranche raises the use of IMF credit to no more than 25 percent of quota. The three subsequent tranches are known as the upper credit tranches. Over time, access to IMF credit substantially above 100 percent of quota under the credit tranches has been permitted; accordingly, the upper credit tranches now refer more generally to any use of IMF credit beyond the first credit tranche. Resources drawn in the credit tranches can be used to meet any balance of payments need.

The segmentation in terms of first and upper credit tranches underscores the basic principle that the IMF requires stronger justification in terms of policy understandings from the member at higher levels of IMF credit outstanding. Conditionality is the mechanism that gives the IMF the needed assurances. The IMF adopts a more liberal attitude in making resources available in the first credit tranche than in the upper credit tranches, provided that the member is making reasonable efforts to solve its balance of payments problems. Requests for use of IMF resources beyond the first credit tranche require substantial justification for the expectation that the member's balance of payments difficulties will be resolved within a reasonable period of time.

Access to the upper credit tranches is normally made under Stand-By Arrangements. These are lines of credit from the IMF under which a "member is assured that it will be able to make purchases from the General Resources Account in accordance with the terms of the decision during a specified period and up to a specified amount."[22] Stand-By Arrangements have long been the core lending instrument of the institution. They were initially intended as precautionary instruments, to be drawn on only if payments difficulties emerged, but have been used more commonly as a source of external financing. Stand-By Arrangements that are treated by members as precautionary, either at the outset of the arrangement or after immediate financing constraints have eased, have again emerged following the opening of world capital markets.

Stand-By Arrangements typically cover a period of 1–1½ years but can be longer, up to a maximum of 3 years. Performance criteria, the phasing of purchases, and program reviews apply to the use of IMF resources in the upper credit tranches, but not in the first credit tranche, even under a Stand-By Arrangement.[23] Repurchases are expected each quarter 2¼–4 years after

---

[22]Article XXX*(b)*.

[23]Outright purchases without IMF arrangements can take place, but are rare.

each purchase, but these expectations can be extended to a maximum repurchase period of 3¼–5 years. In addition to the charges for the use of IMF credit, members pay a commitment fee for Stand-By Arrangements, which is refunded to the extent that amounts under the arrangement are purchased (Table II.2 summarizes the terms of IMF credit under the various policies and facilities).

Extended Fund Facility

The Extended Fund Facility (EFF) was established in 1974 as a vehicle for longer-term external financing for members undertaking needed structural economic reforms. The EFF is designed for economies:
- suffering serious payments imbalances relating to structural maladjustments in production and trade and where price and cost distortions have been widespread, or
- characterized by slow growth and an inherently weak balance of payments position, which prevent pursuit of an active development policy.

The EFF is especially appropriate for members graduating from the Poverty Reduction and Growth Facility (PRGF) programs or transition economies that lack adequate capital market access. At the same time, the EFF and all other IMF facilities are available in principle to any member that meets the eligibility criteria.

Members drawing under the EFF do so in the context of an Extended Arrangement. These are three-year IMF arrangements, which can be extended for a fourth year. Performance criteria and purchases typically follow a semiannual schedule. Repurchases are also made semiannually, and over a longer period than applies to the credit tranches: repurchases are expected 4½–7 years after each purchase but this can be extended to the maximum repurchase period of 4½–10 years. Members pay a refundable commitment fee for Extended Arrangements, as well as the applicable charges for the use of IMF credit.

Supplemental Reserve Facility

The Supplemental Reserve Facility (SRF) was established at the end of 1997, at the height of the Asian financial crisis. Its purpose is to provide financial assistance to members experiencing exceptional balance of payments difficulties due to a large, short-term financing need following a sudden and disruptive loss of confidence reflected in pressure on the capital account and the member's foreign reserves. Access under the SRF is separate from the limits that apply to the credit tranches and the EFF, and it has no explicit limits of its own. SRF resources are provided under Stand-By or Extended Arrangements. The conditionality in an arrangement involving SRF resources is that of the associated Stand-By or Extended Arrangement.

The repurchase period for SRF resources is much shorter than that governing the credit tranches and EFF, reflecting the likelihood of a quicker turnaround in the balance of payments. Repurchases are made in two installments and are expected 1–1½ years after each purchase; this period can be extended up to the maximum repurchase period of 2–2½ years. Resources drawn under the SRF are subject to the basic rate of charge applying to all IMF credit and a specific surcharge. During the first year from the date of the first purchase under the facility, the SRF surcharge is set at 300 basis points, and it rises by 50 basis points at the end of the first year and every six months thereafter, up to a maximum of 500 basis points. The standard commitment fee for Stand-By Arrangements applies.

Contingent Credit Lines

The Contingent Credit Line (CCL) is a new type of lending instrument for the IMF. Conceived in the midst of a series of severe financial crises involving large-scale use of IMF resources by a number of members, the CCL was established by the IMF in 1999 as a means of preventing the spread of capital account–driven crises. The CCL is intended to provide members maintaining strong policies with a precautionary line of defense against balance of payments problems arising from international financial contagion. Although it draws on IMF experience over several decades, the CCL has a number of novel features that set it apart from other IMF lending instruments, notably an element of pre-qualification and automaticity in using IMF resources.

The CCL is subject to demanding eligibility requirements:
- the absence of an immediate need to use IMF resources at the time of approval;
- a positive assessment of policies by the IMF, taking into account the member's adherence to internationally accepted standards (especially the IMF's Special Data Dissemination Standard or SDDS);
- constructive relations with private creditors, with a view to facilitating appropriate involvement of the private sector, and satisfactory management of external vulnerability; and

- a satisfactory economic and financial program, which the member stands ready to adjust as needed.

As with the SRF, CCL resources are provided under Stand-By Arrangements, in combination with credit tranche resources. Access to CCL resources is expected to be in the range of 300–500 percent of quota, and does not count toward the access limits for the credit tranches and the EFF.

Upon approval of an arrangement with CCL resources, a small amount is made available but is not expected to be purchased. If a crisis strikes, the member may request the completion of an activation review, at which the Executive Board would ascertain that the member is affected by a crisis stemming from contagion and that the member's own policies had not been a significant cause of the pressures in its balance of payments. There is a presumption that one-third of the amount committed under the CCL would be released at this time. The phasing and conditionality for the remaining CCL resources would be specified in a post-activation review concluded shortly after or together with the activation review; conditionality would be expected to cover macroeconomic rather than structural policies, given the nature of the balance of payments difficulties.

The financial terms for CCL resources are identical to those governing SRF resources, except that the surcharge on CCL resources over the basic rate of charge is 150 basis points lower: the CCL surcharge is 150 basis points initially, rising by 50 basis points one year after the first purchase and every six months thereafter, up to a maximum surcharge of 350 basis points. The commitment fee for the CCL is the same as for the SRF.

Compensatory Financing Facility

The CFF was the first facility aimed at helping members deal with special balance of payments problems. It was established in the 1960s to ensure timely external financing for members experiencing balance of payments difficulties resulting from a temporary decline in export earnings. A cereal import element was added in 1981; two other elements introduced since the establishment of the CFF have been removed (see Box II.5). In addition to having a balance of payments need related to export shortfalls or excess cereal import costs, the eligibility requirements include the following:

- the export shortfall or excess cereal import cost are of a short-term character;
- the shortfall or excess must be largely attributable to factors beyond the member's control; and

- if the member has balance of payments difficulties beyond the effect of the shortfall or excess, it must have a new or existing arrangement in place at the time of the request for a CFF purchase.

Access under the CFF is subject to its own limits, and does not count toward the access limits under the credit tranches and the EFF. The CFF access limits range from 45 percent of quota for each of the export shortfall and excess cereal import costs elements to a combined limit of 55 percent of quota. Within these limits, actual access is determined by the size of the shortfall or excess, and may be limited by concerns about the member's ability to repay the IMF. Access under the CFF counts toward the threshold for upper credit tranche conditionality—that is, the CFF does not "float" as regards conditionality.[24]

Under certain circumstances, purchases under the CFF may be phased, with purchases subsequent to the initial purchase being conditioned on the member's having an IMF arrangement in place and meeting all the conditions for a purchase or disbursement under that arrangement. They are subject to the same terms as credit tranche resources with respect to charges, repurchase expectations, and repurchase obligations; CFF purchases do not carry a surcharge, however, and do not count toward the calculation of surcharges applying to IMF credit outstanding in excess of 200 percent of quota.

In addition to the time-based early repurchase expectations, the CFF incorporates additional specific early repurchase provisions. If a member makes a purchase on the basis of estimated data for the shortfall in export earnings or excess in cereal import costs, and if the actual data, once they are available, indicate that the purchase exceeded the amount that would have been available had actual data been used, the member is expected to repurchase promptly an amount equivalent to the difference.

Emergency Assistance

The IMF has a long-standing policy of providing financial assistance to members experiencing emergencies. The conditionality associated with IMF lending for this purpose is similar to that required for purchases in the first

---

[24]In practice, this means that a member with 25 percent of quota or more of credit outstanding under the CFF cannot access the credit tranches with first credit tranche (lower) conditionality.

credit tranche. Two basic types of emergencies are covered by this policy: natural disasters, such as earthquakes, floods, or hurricanes; and post-conflict situations, following social disruptions.

Emergency assistance for natural disasters is available where the member cannot meet its immediate financing needs arising from a natural disaster without serious depletion of its foreign reserves. If this exigency were not present, however, IMF assistance for these members could be provided under the CFF or a Stand-By or an Extended Arrangement. The policy conditions include a statement of the general policies the member intends to pursue, and some assurance that the member will cooperate with the IMF in an effort to find, where appropriate, solutions for its balance of payments difficulties.

In post-conflict situations, emergency assistance can be made available where there is an urgent balance of payments need and a role for the IMF in catalyzing support from others, but where the institutional and administrative capacity of the member has been disrupted as a result of social conflict, so that the member is not yet able to develop and implement a comprehensive economic program that could be supported by an IMF arrangement. In these circumstances, there must nevertheless be sufficient capacity for planning and policy implementation and a demonstrated commitment by the authorities. Support from the IMF in these cases must be part of a concerted international effort to address the aftermath of the conflict situation in a comprehensive way.

IMF assistance in emergency situations was initially provided through the flexible application of policies on the use of the credit tranches, but since 2000 has been subject to a special policy outside the credit tranches. Access is normally limited to 25 percent of quota. Larger amounts can be made available on an exceptional basis: a further 25 percent of quota can be provided in post-conflict situations where progress on capacity rebuilding has been slow and the member is not in a position to move to an IMF arrangement after one year but where there is sufficient evidence of the authorities' commitment to reform and capacity to implement policies; tranching of disbursements may be appropriate in these cases. Purchases under emergency assistance are subject to the basic rate of charge and a maximum repurchase period of 3¼–5 years, but are not subject to time-based repurchase expectations and do not count toward the calculation of the surcharge on IMF credit in excess of 200 percent of quota. The IMF has set up a special administered account with the purpose of providing PRGF-eligible countries with post-conflict emergency assistance at the concessional rate of interest of ½ of 1 percent a year (see Appendix III.) To achieve this objective, adequate donor resources will need to be mobilized.

The amounts of IMF credit outstanding by facility during 1990–2000 are shown in Figure II.4.

Currency Holdings

In the balance sheet of the GRA, the IMF distinguishes between usable currencies and other currencies. Usable currencies comprise the currencies of those member countries that have a sufficiently strong balance of payments and reserve positions for their currencies to be used to provide credit to other members. These currency holdings represent the bulk of resources available to meet the future demand for IMF credit. Other currencies include the currencies of members with weaker external positions that are not being used for credit purposes, although they could become usable if the members' balance of payments positions improved, and the currencies of borrowers.

Valuation of Currencies

Currencies and securities held in the GRA's pool of resources are valued in terms of the SDR on the basis of each member's representative rate of exchange. Each member is obligated to maintain, in SDR terms, the value of the balances of the IMF's holdings of its currency in the GRA, but not those held elsewhere by the IMF, such as in the SDA or the Administered Accounts.[25] The total SDR value of the IMF's holdings of currencies in the GRA is kept constant through changes to the amount of members' currency balances. A member has to pay in additional currency if its currency depreciates against the SDR, and the IMF will refund some of these currency holdings if the currency appreciates. This requirement is referred to as the maintenance-of-value obligation. Because of this obligation the IMF's resources are insulated from exchange rate fluctuations.

A member's currency held by the IMF is revalued in SDR terms whenever:
- the currency is used by the IMF in a transaction with another member,
- at the end of the IMF's financial year (April 30),

---

[25]Revaluation changes in members' currencies in relation to the SDR in the other IMF accounts (the SDA and the Administered Accounts) are reported as valuation gains and losses for those accounts.

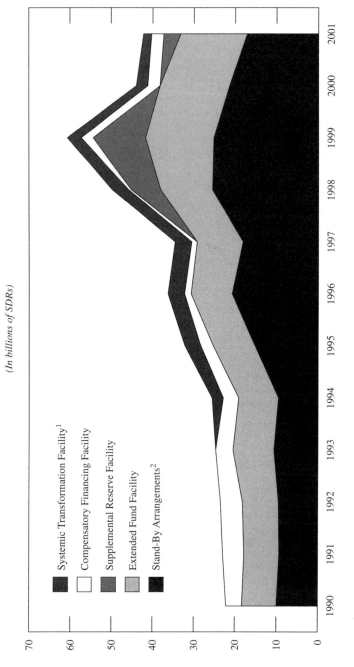

FIGURE II.4. OUTSTANDING IMF CREDIT BY FACILITY, FINANCIAL YEARS ENDED APRIL 30, 1990–2001

(In billions of SDRs)

[1]Credit extended under the 1993–95 Systemic Transformation Facility will not be fully repaid until 2005.
[2]Includes a small amount under the credit tranches and emergency assistance.

48

- at the request of a member during the year, for example, at the end of the member's financial year; and
- on such other occasions as the IMF may decide.

Whenever it becomes necessary to adjust the rate at which the IMF has recorded the use of a member's currency, the new rate becomes effective in the IMF's accounts at the close of business on the date that the new exchange rate is determined. All holdings of a member's currency in the GRA, including any unsettled obligations resulting from an earlier revaluation, are revalued at the new rate. The new rate is applied to all transactions in that currency, including administrative receipts and payments, until such a time as the rate may again need to be adjusted.

The currency valuation adjustments are part of the IMF's holdings of members' currencies. Whenever the IMF revalues its holdings of a member's currency, reflecting a change in its exchange rate with the SDR, an account receivable or an account payable is established for the amount of currency payable by or to the member in order to maintain the value of holdings of the member's currency in terms of the SDR.

SDR Holdings

The IMF does not receive allocations of SDRs, but obtains its SDRs as payment of the reserve asset portion of quota subscriptions and in settlement of charges and, to a lesser degree, repayment of credit. The IMF, in turn, uses these SDRs to pay interest on creditor positions and to provide credit to members. Since SDRs were created as a supplement to existing reserve assets, the IMF does not maintain large holdings of SDRs for long periods of time, but rather recirculates the SDRs it receives back to the membership. The SDR system, and the key role of the GRA in the circulation of SDRs, is discussed in Chapter III.

Gold Holdings

The IMF holds 103 million fine (troy) ounces (3,217 metric tons) of gold at designated official depositories, making it the third largest official holder of gold after the United States and Germany. IMF holdings account for about 10 percent of total official gold stocks. The IMF acquired its gold in various ways (Box II.6). The IMF's gold holdings are valued on its balance sheet on the basis of historical cost, with a book value of SDR 5.9 billion. Valued at end-April 2001 market prices, the IMF's holdings amount to over SDR 21 billion (about $27 billion).

BOX II.6. SOURCES AND USES OF THE IMF'S GOLD

The IMF acquired virtually all its gold holdings through four main types of transactions under the pre-Second Amendment (1978) Articles of Agreement.

• *Subscriptions.* The original Articles of Agreement prescribed that 25 percent of initial subscriptions and quota increases was normally to be paid in gold. This represented the largest source of the IMF's gold.

• *Payment of charges.* Originally, all charges, or interest, on members' outstanding use of IMF credit were normally payable in gold.

• *Repurchases.* Members could use gold to repay the IMF for credit previously extended.

• *Purchases.* A member wishing to obtain the currency of another member could acquire it by selling gold to the IMF. The major use of this provision was sales of gold to the IMF by South Africa in 1970–71.

Outflows of gold from the IMF's holdings occurred under the pre-Second Amendment (1978) Articles of Agreement through sales of gold for currency, and via payment of remuneration and interest. Sales of gold for currency were as follows:

• *Sales for replenishment (1957–70).* In the late 1950s and in the 1960s, the IMF sold gold on several occasions to replenish its holdings of currencies.

• *South African gold and mitigation.* In the early 1970s, the IMF sold gold to members in amounts roughly corresponding to the amounts purchased earlier from South Africa; it also sold gold in connection with payments of gold for quota increases by some members, in order to mitigate the impact of these payments on the gold holdings of reserve centers.

• *Investment in U.S. Government securities (1956–72).* In order to generate income to offset operational deficits, some gold was sold to the United States and the proceeds invested in U.S. Government securities. A significant buildup of reserves through income from charges prompted the IMF to reacquire this gold from the U.S. Government in the early 1970s.

• *Auctions and "restitution" sales (1976–80).* The IMF sold approximately one-third (50 million ounces) of its then-existing gold holdings following an agreement by its members to reduce the role of gold in the international monetary system. Half of this amount was sold in restitution to members at the then-official price of SDR 35 an ounce; the other half was auctioned to the market to finance the Trust Fund, which supported concessional lending by the IMF to low-income countries.

Since 1980, the IMF has had few transactions in gold. A very small amount of gold was received from Cambodia in 1992 in discharge of its overdue obligations. In 1993, the IMF pledged to sell up to 3 million ounces of gold if the resources of the PRGF Trust Reserve Account were insufficient to cover repayments to PRGF creditors resulting from loans made to encash rights under the rights accumulation approach. Finally, during 1999–2000, the IMF conducted a series of off-market transactions in gold that left its gold holdings unchanged, in order to generate resources to help finance its participation in the HIPC Initiative.

Gold in the Articles of Agreement

Before the Second Amendment of the Articles in April 1978, the role of gold in the IMF and in the international monetary system was central and pervasive. The Second Amendment contained a number of provisions that, in combination, were intended to achieve a gradual reduction of the role of gold in the international monetary system and in the IMF. The Second Amendment:

- eliminated the use of gold as the common denominator of the par value system and as the basis of the value of the SDR;
- abolished the official price of gold and abolished the obligatory uses of gold in transactions between the IMF and its members;
- required the IMF, in its dealings in gold, to avoid managing its price or establishing a fixed price of gold; and
- included an undertaking by members to collaborate with the IMF and other members with respect to reserve assets to promote better international surveillance of international liquidity.

The Articles now limit the use of gold in the IMF's transactions. Any transactions in gold by the IMF require a decision by an 85 percent majority of the total voting power in the IMF. The IMF:

- may sell gold outright on the basis of prevailing market prices;
- may accept gold in the discharge of a member's obligations to the IMF at an agreed price on the basis of prices in the market at the time of acceptance;
- does not have the authority to engage in any other gold transactions, for example, loans, leases, swaps, or use of gold as collateral; and
- does not have the authority to buy gold.

The IMF's Policy on Gold

The IMF's policies on gold are governed by the following five principles:

- As an undervalued asset held by the IMF, gold provides fundamental strength to its balance sheet. Any mobilization of IMF gold should avoid weakening its overall financial position.
- Gold holdings provide the IMF with operational maneuverability both as regards the use of its resources and through adding credibility to its precautionary balances. In these respects, the benefits of the IMF's gold holdings are passed on to the membership at large, including both creditors and debtors.

- The IMF should continue to hold a relatively large amount of gold among its assets, not only for prudential reasons, but also to meet unforeseen contingencies.
- The IMF has a systemic responsibility to avoid causing disruptions to the functioning of the gold market.
- Profits from any gold sales should be retained in an investment fund, and only the investment income should be used for any purposes that may be agreed upon by the IMF members.

The IMF's Gold Since 1980

Uses of the IMF's gold have occurred on two occasions since 1980 without changing the IMF's long-term holdings of gold. As was the case with the open-market auctions of gold in 1976–80, these uses of gold were for the benefit of the poorest members of the IMF. Toward this end, the IMF pledged gold in 1993 and decided in 1999 to conduct off-market transactions of gold.

Gold Pledge

To reassure creditors to the Enhanced Structural Adjustment Facility (ESAF) that they would be repaid for ESAF (now PRGF) loans made to encash rights under the "rights accumulation approach," it was agreed, if necessary, to mobilize some of the IMF's gold. For this purpose, in 1993 the IMF decided — with the required 85 percent majority of the total voting power — to sell up to 3 million ounces of gold if it were determined that the resources in the PRGF Trust Reserve Account (plus other available means of financing) were insufficient to meet payments to be made from that account to PRGF creditors. The shortfall would be covered by gold sales to the extent of previous drawings on the Reserve Account attributable to overdue repayments by borrowers of loans for the encashment of rights, plus the interest earnings forgone on such drawings.

It is difficult to assess the likelihood that the gold pledge for rights encashments under PRGF arrangements would be drawn on in the future, mainly because of uncertainty about future borrowings under the rights approach. Sierra Leone and Zambia still have loans outstanding to the PRGF Trust under the rights approach, but these loans are rapidly diminishing either because they are coming close to maturity or because they are covered under the enhanced HIPC Initiative. It is, therefore, highly unlikely that the gold pledge would be activated in connection with these loans. Moreover, the gold pledge could not be called upon until after the resources of the Reserve Account of the PRGF Trust were exhausted.[26] Nevertheless, three countries—Liberia, Somalia, and Sudan—remain eligible for the rights approach and could conceivably borrow sizable sums from the PRGF in connection with rights encashments at some time in the future, provided the Executive Board continues to extend the availability of the rights approach. Whether these countries will follow the rights approach to arrears clearance is uncertain. In any case, the earliest rights encashments could not take place for a few years and repayment of those PRGF loans would only commence five and half years after such disbursements.

Off-Market Transactions in Gold

To help finance its contribution to the HIPC Initiative, the IMF in 1999–2000 conducted a series of off-market transactions in gold. During December 1999–April 2000, the IMF sold a total of 12.944 million fine ounces of gold to Brazil and Mexico at the prevailing market price on the day of each transaction. The total amount sold was equivalent to SDR 2.7 billion ($3.7 billion). After each sale, the gold was immediately accepted back by the IMF at the same price in settlement of financial obligations of these members to the IMF. The net effect of these transactions left the IMF's holdings of physical gold unchanged, but the gold accepted back was included in the IMF's balance sheet at the market price of the transactions, instead of at the original price of SDR 35 a fine ounce.

In accordance with the Articles, the equivalent of SDR 35 a fine ounce from the proceeds of the sales was retained in the GRA. The proceeds in excess of this amount (totaling SDR 2.2 billion, or about $2.9 billion) are held in the SDA and invested. The income from these investments, which will be transferred to the PRGF-HIPC Trust when needed, will be used to help finance the IMF's contribution to the HIPC Initiative. In this context, the Board of Governors of the IMF adopted a resolution in September 1999 stating that the off-market gold transactions would "be a one-time operation of a highly exceptional nature."

These gold transactions affected the IMF's balance sheet and income as follows:

---

[26]The Reserve Account of the PRGF Trust is discussed in Chapter IV.

- The IMF's holdings of usable currencies in the GRA were lower, and reserve tranche positions higher, than they would otherwise have been by the amount of profit (SDR 2.2 billion). This is because Brazil and Mexico paid in gold instead of usable currencies, which would have been used to reduce reserve tranche positions of creditor members.
- The IMF's net income is affected by the remuneration expense on the continuing enlarged reserve tranche positions. The additional remuneration expense varies with the rate of remuneration, and amounted to an estimated SDR 94 million in FY2001. For comparison, the IMF's net income target for FY2001, the first year in which the full income effect of the off-market gold transactions was felt, was SDR 48 million, and for FY2002 net income is targeted at SDR 51 million.

While the transactions were successful in that they allowed the IMF to contribute to the resolution of the debt problems of the HIPCs, they resulted in an increase in the IMF's cost of operations. Since, under standard procedures (see the discussion of "Operational Income" below), this relatively large increase in cost would have resulted in a higher rate of charge, the cost increase was mitigated or offset through the existing burden-sharing mechanism and placed in the SCA-1. In the same way, SDR 94 million is being generated in FY2002.

The Resource and Liability Side

Quotas

Each member of the IMF is assigned a quota and pays a capital subscription to the IMF that is equal to its quota. As noted earlier, a quarter of a member's quota subscription is normally paid in reserve assets, with the remainder paid in the member's own currency.[27] Quotas are expressed in SDRs and their size is determined by the IMF's Board of Governors, broadly on the basis of the economic size of the country, and taking into account quotas of similar countries. To help in this determination, five formulas are used that relate the quota to the size of the country's GDP, current account transactions, and official reserves. As of April 30, 2001, total quotas

---

[27]The IMF has made arrangements to assist members with insufficient reserves to pay the reserve asset portion of their quota subscription payment through a same-day, no-cost IMF lending operation (see Chapter III, Box III.4).

of all members amounted to SDR 212.4 billion. A list of members and their quotas is provided in Appendix I.

Members' quotas constitute the financial base of the IMF and determine its size, as well as serve other functions as determined by the IMF's Articles.

- Quotas provide the vast bulk of reserve assets that can be used in the provision of foreign reserves by the IMF, despite the availability of borrowed resources and the growing role of administered resources to provide concessional assistance to the IMF's poorest members.
- Quotas determine the distribution of voting power in the IMF.[28] Quotas determine members' financial relationships with the IMF and, through the effect on voting power, members' roles in IMF decision-making and representation on the Executive Board. Many decisions are taken by a simple majority vote, though special voting majorities are required for some important financial decisions (Appendix II).
- Quotas continue to play a crucial role in determining the demand for IMF resources. Quotas serve as the basis for access to such resources in the great majority of IMF-supported programs, subject to limits set by the Articles and the Executive Board.[29] Over the years, however, the relationship between quotas and access has become more elastic, especially as the demand for IMF resources has become more unpredictable because of the increased role of capital flows in balance of payments disequilibria. Waivers of the Articles' limits on access to IMF resources have been granted where necessary to allow access in line with operational requirements.
- Quotas also determine a member's share in a general allocation of SDRs.[30]

The initial quotas of the original members of the IMF were determined at the Bretton Woods conference in 1944 (Schedule A of the IMF Articles); those of subsequent members have been determined by the IMF's Board of

---

[28]A member's voting power is equal to 250 basic votes plus one additional vote for each SDR 100,000 in quota. Basic votes therefore help to strengthen the relative voting power of members with smaller quotas.

[29]While the IMF's holdings of a member's currency, which measure its access to IMF credit, are restricted to no more than 200 percent of quota under the Articles (Article V, Section 3(b)(iii)), this limit—which amounts to IMF credit of 100 percent of quota—is routinely waived. See the discussion of "Access Policy" above.

[30]Article XVIII, Section 2(b).

Governors, based on principles consistent with those applied to existing members. The IMF has adjusted quotas within the context of five-yearly general reviews and on an ad hoc basis outside of general reviews. An 85 percent majority of voting power is needed to change quotas.

The determination of the quota of a new member of the IMF is based on the principle that a member's quota should be in the same range as the quotas of existing members of comparable economic size and characteristics. Operationally, this principle has been applied through the use of quota formulas. Since the IMF's inception, the calculated quotas derived from the quota formulas have been used to help guide decisions regarding the size and distribution of members' actual quotas.

Quota formulas have evolved over time starting from the formula — containing national income, official reserves, imports, export variability, and the ratio of exports to national income — that was devised at Bretton Woods in 1944 to give support to the broad configuration of initial quotas that was being negotiated.

A multiformula approach was adopted in the early 1960s, when the Bretton Woods formula was revised and supplemented by four other formulas containing the same basic variables but with larger weights for external trade and export variability. The Bretton Woods formula, with its relatively high weight for national income, has generally favored large economies, while the additional four formulas have tended to produce higher quotas than the Bretton Woods formula for smaller, more open economies. The five formulas, which are listed in Box II.7, were last modified in 1982–83.

General Reviews

The IMF conducts general reviews of all members' quotas normally at five year intervals.[31] Such reviews allow the IMF to assess the adequacy of quotas in terms of members' needs for conditional liquidity and the IMF's ability to finance those needs. A general review also allows for adjustments of members' quotas to reflect changes in their relative positions in the world economy. Of the general reviews conducted to date, only one (in 1958/59) was outside the five-year cycle.

The main issues addressed in general quota reviews are the size of an overall increase in quotas and the distribution of the increase among the

---

[31]Article III, Section 2(a).

BOX II.7. THE PRESENT FIVE QUOTA FORMULAS

The present five quota formulas, with the Bretton Woods formula listed first, are:

$$CQ = (0.01Y + 0.025R + 0.05P + 0.2276VC)(1 + C/Y),$$

$$CQ = (0.0065Y + 0.0205125R + 0.078P + 0.4052VC)(1 + C/Y),$$

$$CQ = (0.0045Y + 0.03896768R + 0.07P + 0.76976VC)(1 + C/Y),$$

$$CQ = 0.005Y + 0.042280464R + 0.044\,(P + C) + 0.8352VC,$$

$$CQ = 0.0045Y + 0.05281008R + 0.039\,(P + C) + 1.0432VC,$$

where CQ = calculated quota;

Y = GDP at current market prices for a recent year;

R = twelve-month average of gold and foreign exchange reserves, including SDR holdings and reserve positions in the IMF, for a recent year;

P = annual average of current payments (goods, services, income, and private transfers) for a recent five-year period;

C = annual average of current receipts (goods, services, income, and private transfers) for a recent five-year period; and

VC = variability of current receipts, defined as one standard deviation from the five-year moving average centered on the third year, for a recent 13-year period.

For each of the four non–Bretton Woods formulas, quota calculations are multiplied by an adjustment factor so that the sum of the calculations across members equals that derived from the Bretton Woods formula. The calculated quota of a member is the higher of the Bretton Woods calculation or the average of the lowest two of the remaining four calculations (after adjustment).

57

members. Four reviews concluded that no increase in quotas was needed. In the other eight reviews, the overall quota increase ranged from 31 percent to 61 percent (Tables II.3 and II.4).

Increases in members' quotas during general reviews typically consist of two elements: (1) an equiproportional element which is distributed to all members according to their existing quota shares; and (2) a selective element which is distributed to either all members or a subset of members. The selective element is used to attain a change in quota shares among members. For any overall increase in quotas, the larger the selective increase, the greater the redistribution of quota shares. In practice, the selective component has tended to be relatively small.

Both the list of members eligible for a selective increase and the way of distributing the selective element are based on the Executive Board's judgment. The distribution of selective quota increases have generally been based on calculated quotas.[32] Calculated quotas are determined by the quota formulas, which have been designed to provide a quantified measure of a country's relative economic position.[33] The following examples illustrate the methods used.

- During the Sixth Review in 1976, the Executive Board decided to double the quota share of the major oil exporters with the stipulation that the collective share of all the developing countries should not fall. The decision was based on the judgment that such a reallocation would strengthen the IMF's liquidity. In this instance, the quota formulas played no role in identifying the members eligible for the selective increase.

- Under the Eleventh Review in 1998, 25 percent of the quota increase was selective. The quota formulas helped determine each member's share of the selective increase as follows: (1) 15 percent of the total increase (three-fifths of the selective element) was distributed to all members; (2) in addition, 10 percent of the total increase was distributed

---

[32]Since the Eighth Review in 1982/83, all members have received an increase comprised of an equiproportional element and a selective element that reflected a member's share in calculated quotas.

[33]As further explained below, formulas are one element in determining actual quotas. While quota formulas are not mentioned in the Articles, and the Executive Board has not formally adopted any formula, the Board has usually relied on them as an independent measure of members' relative economic position in the world economy. Typically, the quota resulting from the formulas—the calculated quota—is different from the actual quota of a member and, in the most recent review, actual quotas were on average less than half of calculated quotas.

TABLE II.3. GENERAL REVIEWS OF IMF QUOTAS
(In percent)

Review of Quotas	Board of Governors' Adoption of Resolution	Equiproportional Increase in Quotas[1]	Overall Increase in Quotas	Entry into Effect
First Quinquennial	No increase proposed	—	—	
Second Quinquennial	No increase proposed	—	—	
1958/59	February 2, 1959 and April 6, 1959[2]	50	60.7	April 6, 1959
Third Quinquennial	No increase proposed	—	—	
Fourth Quinquennial	March 31, 1965	25	30.7	February 23, 1966
Fifth General	February 9, 1970	25	35.4	October 30, 1970
Sixth General	March 22, 1976	Increases were determined on the basis of different groups of countries	33.6	April 1, 1978
Seventh General	December 11, 1978	50	50.9	November 29, 1980
Eighth General	March 31, 1983	19	47.5	November 30, 1983
Ninth General	June 28, 1990	30	50.0	November 11, 1992
Tenth General	No increase proposed	—	—	
Eleventh General	January 30, 1998	33.75	45.0	January 22, 1999

[1]Uniform percentage increase for all members participating in the review.
[2]The February 1959 resolution provided for an equiproportional increase of 50 percent and special increases for 3 countries; the resolution adopted in April 1959 provided for special increases for 14 additional countries.

TABLE II.4. CHANGES IN IMF QUOTAS
(Quotas in millions of SDRs)[1]

Year	IMF Membership (1)	Proposed Quotas (2)	New members[2] Number (3)	New members[2] Quotas (4)	General reviews[3] (5)	Ad hoc and other (6)	Total[4] (7)
1944[5]	40	7,514.00	40	7,514.00	—	—	—
1950	49	8,036.50	10	649.50	—	-2.00[6]	522.50
			(1)	(125.00)			
1955	58	8,750.50	10	837.00	—	2.00[6]	714.00
			(1)	(125.00)			
1959	69	14,640.25	11	404.50	5,328.75	156.50[7]	5,889.75
1965	102	20,932.00	34	756.75	4,791.75	793.25	6,291.75
			(1)	(50.00)			
1970	116	28,776.00	14	204.25	7,393.50	246.25	7,844.00
1976	133	38,976.40	17	445.40	9,755.00	—	10,200.40
1978	141	59,605.50	8	140.10	19,839.00	650.00	20,629.10
1983	146	89,236.30	5	394.40	28,176.50	1,059.90	29,630.80
1990	154	135,214.70[8]	10	1,016.75	45,082.15	—	45,978.40
			(2)	(120.50)			
1998	183[9]	212,029.00	31	12,736.65	65,802.95	40.00	76,814.30
			(2)	(1,765.30)			
2001	183	213,711.00	—	—	—	1,682.00[10]	1,682.00

[1]Quotas in the IMF were expressed in U.S. dollars at the equivalent of the 1934 official gold price until the Sixth General Review of Quotas in 1976, when the IMF's unit of account had switched to the SDR, again valued at the 1934 official gold price. Consequently, the U.S. dollar and SDR, through 1970, are directly comparable at an exchange rate of SDR 1 = US$1.

[2]Countries that withdrew from membership or whose memberships were conferred to successor countries are shown in parentheses.

[3]As of the dates of adoption of Board of Governors' resolutions proposing adjustments in members' quotas.

[4]Sum of columns (4), (5), and (6).

[5]Excluding Australia, Haiti, Liberia, New Zealand, and the U.S.S.R., which did not join the IMF at the time of the Bretton Woods Agreement (see Schedule A of the Articles of Agreement), and including increases agreed for Egypt, France, the Islamic Republic of Iran, and Paraguay shortly after the IMF began operations.

[6]The quota of Honduras was reduced at its request for 1948 but was restored to the original amount in 1951.

[7]Includes SDR 121.0 million of special allocations for countries with small quotas.

[8]Includes Cambodia, which did not participate in the Ninth General Review.

[9]Includes the Federal Republic of Yugoslavia, which had not yet succeeded to IMF membership. On December 20, 2000 the Executive Board of the IMF determined that the Federal Republic of Yugoslavia had fulfilled the necessary conditions to succeed to membership in the IMF.

[10]Ad hoc increase for China.

to those countries whose ratio of calculated to actual quotas was considered to be most "out of line."[34]

Adjustments of quota shares have tended to take place within general reviews, usually in the context of an urgent need for additional resources on the part of the IMF. This reflects the fact that it has been easier to reach agreement if all members receive an increase in quotas. Agreement is more difficult to reach when only a subset of members receives an increase, as the quotas of all other members would remain unchanged and their quota shares would decline.

Ad Hoc Increases

A member can request an adjustment of its quota at any time.[35] Ad hoc quota increases can occur both within and outside the context of a general review. In recent years, they have tended to occur within a general review. As with selective increases, both the quota formulas and the Executive Board's judgment have played a role in determining the amount of the ad hoc adjustment. The following are examples.

- Five members (France, the Islamic Republic of Iran, Egypt, Paraguay, and the Philippines) received ad hoc increases between 1947 and 1959. The main factor underlying these increases was the view that the initial quotas of these members at the time of the Bretton Woods conference in 1945 had been set at unduly low levels. Between 1959 and 1969, the quotas of another nine countries were adjusted on an ad hoc basis. All of the foregoing increases occurred outside the context of a general review.
- Japan received an ad hoc increase under the Ninth Review. In this case, the seven largest industrial countries agreed to redistribute quota increases among themselves in such a manner that the quota increases for the rest of the membership were not affected.[36]

---

[34]"Out of line" was defined as those countries with ratios of calculated to actual quotas above one. Thirty-eight members met this criterion. Five of these members, whose quotas were farthest out of line and which were able to contribute to the IMF's liquidity over the medium term, received 1 percent of the 10 percent share going to the group of 38 members.

[35]Under Article III, Section 2*(a)*, the IMF may, "if it thinks fit, consider at any other time the adjustment of any particular quota at the request of the member concerned."

[36]As a result of this redistribution to accommodate an ad hoc increase in the quota of Japan, the new quotas for Germany and Japan were equalized, as were the quotas of France and the United Kingdom (ranked just below those of Japan and Germany), and adjustments were made to the quotas of the United States, Canada, and Italy so that the total quotas for the seven countries as a group was maintained unchanged.

Since 1970, there have been only four ad hoc increases in quotas outside the framework of a general review. Ad hoc increases in the quotas of China in 1980 and of Cambodia in 1994 were associated with the change in representation of the member in the IMF (China) and the resumption of active relations with the IMF (Cambodia), as China's initial quota had never been increased and Cambodia's quota had not been increased since 1970. Saudi Arabia received an ad hoc increase in 1981. A major factor underlying Saudi Arabia's ad hoc increase was the desire to strengthen the IMF's liquidity position during the developing country debt crisis before the Eighth Review had been completed. China also received an ad hoc quota increase in 2001 to better reflect its position in the world economy following its resumption of exercising sovereignty over Hong Kong. For each of the post-1969 cases, the quota formulas played a role in determining the extent of the ad hoc increase.

Role of the Quota Formulas

In practice, the role of the quota formulas in determining actual quotas and quota share adjustments has been quite limited. As noted above, quota increases in the context of general reviews have been distributed largely on the basis of a uniform proportionate increase in actual quotas. The continuing significant difference between actual and calculated quota shares reflects:

- the Executive Board's view that general quota reviews should provide all members with an adequate increase in quota;
- a general reluctance to make politically difficult quota share adjustments; and
- widespread dissatisfaction with formulas that were viewed as overly complex, lacking in transparency, and not representative of actual conditions in the world economy.

In 1999, the IMF established an external panel of independent experts, the Quota Formula Review Group (QFRG), to assess the adequacy of the formulas used to guide the determination of quotas and to make recommendations for reforms that would take account of changes in the world economy and the international financial system and the increasing globalization of markets. The eight member panel, chaired by Professor Richard Cooper of Harvard University, submitted a report that was considered by the Executive

Board, along with a staff commentary, in August 2000. The report and staff commentary were subsequently published on the IMF's website.[37]

The QFRG report provided information about the history and operation of the quota formulas, suggested guiding principles for future reforms, and presented recommendations to simplify and update the formulas. The Executive Board discussion revealed a wide range of views on the issues raised in the report and the staff commentary. There was general recognition of the need to simplify the present formulas and to update them to take account of the growing role of capital flows. However, concern was expressed that a preliminary partial quantification of the formula recommended by the panel pointed toward a greater concentration of quotas among the largest industrial countries (subsequently confirmed by more complete and updated staff calculations).[38] Executive Directors agreed on the need to carry forward the work of the external panel with a view to developing quota formulas that more fully reflect members' roles in the world economy. The International Monetary and Financial Committee (IMFC) supported this view at their meeting in Prague in September 2001, and a work program has been adopted to further consider alternative quota formulas prior to the 2001 Annual Meetings.

Reserve Tranche Positions

In making the reserve asset portion of their quota payment, members acquire a liquid claim on the IMF in exchange for the reserves they provide, much like a demand deposit in a commercial bank. This claim is called the reserve tranche position; it is equal to the member's quota less the IMF's holdings of the member's currency in the GRA (excluding currency holdings that stem from the member's own use of credit). The share of a member's subscription maintained in reserve assets varies over time from its initial level of some 25 percent at the time of quota payment. A member's reserve tranche position increases when the IMF uses its currency to lend to other members, and decreases when borrowing members use the currency to make repayments. Reserve tranche positions are part of members' liquid international reserves because a member may, subject only to its representation of a balance of payments need, convert its SDR-denominated reserve asset into

---

[37]See http://www.imf.org/external/np/tre/quota/2000/eng/qfrg/report/index.htm and http://www.imf.org/external/np/tre/quota/2000/eng/qfrg/comment/index.htm.

[38]See http://www.imf.org/external/np/tre/quota/2001/eng/erqfq.htm.

one or more freely usable currencies by drawing on the IMF (Box II.8). A member is obligated, if necessary, to provide an amount of reserve assets of up to 100 percent of its quota. The amount of reserve assets provided to the IMF has in practice fallen well below this maximum (Figure II.5).

The IMF pays interest, called remuneration, on a member's reserve position in the IMF, except on a small portion that is provided to the IMF as an interest-free resource. This unremunerated (non-interest-bearing) portion of the reserve tranche position is equal to 25 percent of the member's quota on April 1, 1978—that part of the quota that was paid in gold prior to the Second Amendment of the IMF's Articles. The gold tranche was never remunerated historically, so it was natural to set aside this same amount in terms of SDRs on this date as the unremunerated reserve tranche. For a member that joined the IMF after that date, the unremunerated reserve tranche is the same percentage of its initial quota as the average unremunerated reserve tranche was as a percentage of the quotas of all other members when the new member joined the IMF. The unremunerated reserve tranche remains fixed for each member in nominal terms, but because of subsequent quota increases, it is now significantly lower when expressed as a percentage of quota.[39] The average is equal to 3.8 percent, but the actual percentage is different for each member.

Precautionary Balances

The IMF's resources in the GRA increase through additions to its precautionary balances, which comprise reserves and balances that have been set aside in the first Special Contingent Account (SCA-1). The level and rate of accumulation of precautionary balances reflect the IMF's assessment of the risk of future operational deficits and general credit risk, including that aris-

---

[39]In the past, the proportion of the reserve tranche that was remunerated was sometimes related to the concept of the "norm" for remuneration, which was calculated as the total of (1) 75 percent of a member's quota before the Second Amendment, plus (2) any subsequent increases in quota. For a country that became a member after April 1, 1978, the norm is a percentage of its quota equal to the weighted average relative to quota of the norms applicable to all other members on the date that the member joined the IMF, plus the amounts of any increases in its quota afterward. At each quota increase, a member's norm rises, becoming closer to 100 percent of its quota. The remunerated reserve tranche excludes certain holdings: all currency holdings acquired when the member used IMF resources, and currency holdings in the IMF No. 2 Account that are less than $1/10$ of 1 percent of the member's quota. See the section on "IMF Accounts in Member Countries."

BOX II.8. RESERVE TRANCHE POLICIES

The reserve tranche can be considered as the "facility of first resort." It stands apart from the credit tranches and the various facilities in that a member's reserve tranche position is part of its own foreign exchange reserves. Purchases in the reserve tranche do not therefore constitute use of IMF credit. To preserve this character as a reserve asset available at the discretion of the member, the IMF has adopted reserve tranche policies:

- The definition of the reserve tranche (quota less holdings of the member's currency) explicitly excludes currency holdings arising from past use of IMF credit. This is intended to enable members to make purchases in the credit tranches without having first to use their reserve tranche. The member can choose which resources to use first.

- Purchases in the reserve tranche are subject to a representation by the member of a balance of payments need, as with any use of IMF resources, but the member's representation of need cannot be challenged by the IMF.

- Reserve tranche purchases are not subject to conditionality, charges, or repurchase expectations and obligations.

---

ing from overdue obligations and the risk that debtor members in good standing might at some point fall into arrears. This latter risk increases with the level and concentration of outstanding credit, but is contained by the positive economic effects of members' adjustment policies and the IMF's preferred creditor status. Reserves also provide a small amount of liquidity in the GRA. The level and composition of the precautionary balances in the GRA in recent years are shown in Table II.5.

Reserves reflect accumulated net income and comprise the Special Reserve and the General Reserve. Resources in the Special Reserve may be used for any purpose for which resources in the General Reserve may be used, except distribution.

- The Special Reserve was established in 1957, initially with the proceeds from a gold investment program, to provide safeguards against operational deficits that were subsequently charged against this reserve. Additions to the Special Reserve have since been financed from net income, other than income derived from the SRF.

- The General Reserve was established in 1958 to meet capital losses or administrative deficits. From FY1998, SRF net income has been placed

FIGURE II.5. AVERAGE RESERVE POSITION OF MEMBERS IN THE
FINANCIAL TRANSACTIONS PLAN, JANUARY 1990–APRIL 2001

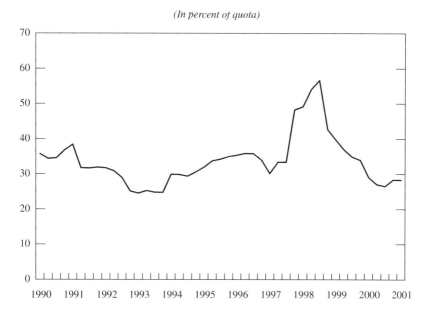

(In percent of quota)

in the General Reserve, which is the only income placed in this reserve since 1971. Any distribution of the General Reserve must be made to all members in proportion to their quotas.

Special Contingent Accounts (SCAs) are established and balances accumulated as part of the IMF's overall strategy to protect itself against the negative financial impact of protracted arrears, that is, obligations that have remained overdue for at least six months.[40] The SCA-1 was established in 1987 as a safeguard against potential losses resulting from an ultimate failure of members in protracted arrears to settle their financial obligations to the IMF. After an initial placement of SDR 26.5 million of excess income in that year, annual additions to the SCA-1 have been generated through "burden-

---

[40]The IMF also levies special charges on repurchases and charges overdue for less than six months. See Chapter V, "Protecting the IMF's Financial Position."

TABLE II.5. LEVEL OF PRECAUTIONARY BALANCES IN THE GRA

	End of Financial Year					
	1996	1997	1998	1999	2000[1]	2001[1]
	(In billions of SDRs)					
Reserves	1.9	2.0	2.1	2.6	2.8	3.0
SCA-1	0.7	0.8	0.9	1.0	1.1	1.2
SCA-2[2]	0.9	1.0	1.0	1.0	—	—
Precautionary balances	3.5	3.8	4.0	4.6	3.9	4.2
Less: credit in arrears	−1.1	−1.1	−1.0	−1.0	−1.0	−0.9
SCA-2[2]	−0.9	−1.0	−1.0	−1.0	—	—
Free reserves	1.5	1.7	2.0	2.6	2.9	3.3
	(In percent)					
Free reserves as a percentage of credit in good standing	4.2	5.1	4.1	4.3	7.0	8.0
Precautionary balances as a percentage of total credit outstanding	9.7	10.9	8.1	7.5	9.0	10.0

[1]Excludes cumulative effects of change in accounting method in FY2000.
[2]See Box II.9.

sharing" adjustments to the rate of charge and the rate of remuneration (Box II.9). These allocations have amounted to 5 percent of GRA reserves at the beginning of the year up until FY2001, when the allocation was reduced to 3.3 percent. Balances in the SCA-1 are refundable to the contributing debtor and creditor member countries when all overdue obligations have been settled, or earlier if the IMF so decides.[41]

The IMF's objective to date has been to maintain a level of total precautionary balances at least equal to credit to members in protracted arrears, a goal that was first achieved in FY1993, and which has since been maintained.

---

[41]A second Special Contingent Account (SCA-2) was established as a safeguard against possible losses arising from purchases made through the encashment of rights accumulated under a rights accumulation program (RAP), and to provide additional liquidity for the financing of those encashments (see Box II.9 and Chapter V). SCA-2 was terminated in 1999.

BOX II.9. THE BURDEN-SHARING MECHANISM

Since 1986, the burden-sharing mechanism has made up for the loss of income from unpaid charges and has been used to accumulate resources in two Special Contingent Accounts (SCAs). The mechanism works by providing for additions and deductions to the rates of charge and remuneration, respectively.

Resources collected from individual members under the mechanism are refundable to them as arrears cases are resolved, or as may be decided by the IMF. Thus, resources collected for unpaid charges are refunded when these charges are eventually settled. At end-April 2001, cumulative deferred charges that were subject to burden sharing amounted to SDR 1,796 million and settlements of unpaid charges of SDR 993 million had been made and refunded.

Of the two Special Contingent Accounts, the first, SCA-1, was established specifically to protect against the financial impact of arrears in general. The second, SCA-2, collected resources (1) to finance the encashment of "rights" earned by eligible members in arrears to later draw on IMF resources, and (2) to safeguard against the risk of loss arising from purchases made in connection with the encashment of rights. SCA-2 was terminated in 1999, and the balances in the account refunded, after it was concluded that other precautionary balances in the GRA provided adequate protection against the risks associated with rights-related credit. The termination of SCA-2 was also part of an overall agreement on the financing of the PRGF (then ESAF) and HIPC initiatives, for which it was envisaged that some members would voluntarily contribute resources refunded from SCA-2.

In the aggregate, creditor and debtor members have contributed equal amounts for unpaid charges and for allocations to the SCA-1, whereas creditors provided three-fourths of the amounts contributed to the SCA-2. A total of SDR 1.2 billion had been accumulated in the SCA-1 at end-April 2001. A total of SDR 1 billion was accumulated during the operation of the SCA-2 in 1990–97.

In addition, to protect itself against general credit risk, the IMF has established a target for precautionary balances in excess of overdue credit. The target range for these "free reserves" is 3–5 percent of the amount of outstanding "credit in good standing." Free reserves had risen to 8.0 percent of credit in good standing at end-April 2001 (see Table II.5).

Income and Expenses

The amount added to reserves each year is the net income resulting from the difference between operational income and operational and administrative expenses.

Virtually all of the IMF's operational income is derived from the charges (interest on loans) that are levied on the outstanding use of credit in the GRA. In addition to the basic rate of charge (i.e., the rate of charge before burden sharing), the use of IMF credit under certain circumstances is subject to surcharges, and all IMF credit is subject to service charges, commitment fees on credit lines, and special charges (see Table II.2).[42] A small amount of income is also generated by receipts of interest on the IMF's SDR holdings (as explained in Chapter III).

Operational expenses consist of the remuneration (interest) paid on remunerated reserve tranche positions, the allocation to the SCA-1, and the payment of interest on outstanding IMF borrowing, if any. Net operational income (operational income less operational expenses) is used to cover the IMF's administrative expenses, and the remainder constitutes net income (Table II.6).[43]

Operational Income

The IMF aims to achieve a target level of net income each financial year to add to its reserves.[44] Based on the net income target, the SDR interest rate, projected credit, and the outlook for administrative expenses, the IMF estimates the basic rate of charge that is necessary to achieve the income target.[45] The basic rate is set for the year as a proportion of the SDR interest rate. For FY2001, this proportion was set at 115.9 percent.

---

[42]The IMF also has access to a relatively small amount of interest-free resources, including its precautionary balances and the unremunerated portion of reserve tranche positions of members.

[43]The Income Statement of the General Department also includes the income of the SDA, which is discussed later in this chapter.

[44]The annual increase in reserves was set as 3 percent of reserves in the GRA at the beginning of the year for financial years 1981–84, 5 percent for financial years 1985–99, 3.9 percent for financial year 2000, and 1.7 percent for financial years 2001–02. These figures exclude income from surcharges.

[45]The procedure setting the basic rate of charge is governed by Rule I-6(4).

TABLE II.6. INCOME STATEMENT OF THE GENERAL DEPARTMENT,
FINANCIAL YEAR ENDED APRIL 30, 2001
(In millions of SDRs)

GRA operational income	
Interest and charges	2,207.1
Interest on SDR holdings	112.5
Other charges and income	68.7
	2,388.3
GRA operational expenses	
Remuneration and financing costs	1,734.3
Allocation to SCA-1	94.0
	1,828.3
GRA administrative expenses	384.6
Net GRA income	175.5
SDA income	
Income earned on investments	150.0
Interest on loans	1.4
Net SDA income	151.4

Note: Numbers may not add to totals due to rounding.

A separate midyear review is undertaken to establish whether an adjustment to the basic rate of charge is required in view of developments during the year.

At the end of the financial year, if net income exceeds the amount projected at the beginning of the year, the Executive Board has, in recent years, decided to reduce the rate of charge retroactively. Alternatively, the Board can decide to:

- place all or part of any excess to reserves; or
- make a distribution of excess income to members; or
- take the excess into account to lower the net income target for the subsequent financial year.

When net income falls short of the target, the Executive Board has generally decided to increase the rate of charge in the subsequent financial year to make up for the shortfall.

Operational Expenses

The IMF pays remuneration (interest) on members' reserve tranche positions equal to the SDR interest rate, except on a small portion, as indicated earlier (see section on "Reserve Tranche Positions").[46] Remuneration payments account for almost all of IMF operational expenses when there is no outstanding IMF borrowing. If borrowing is outstanding, the IMF also pays interest on it. The interest rate on borrowing under the General Arrangements to Borrow (GAB) is equal to the SDR interest rate, while under the New Arrangements to Borrow (NAB), it may be equal to or higher than the SDR interest rate, as explained below under "Borrowing."

Administrative Expenses

The IMF's administrative expenses can be divided into personnel, travel, building occupancy, and other such costs. Personnel and travel-related outlays typically account for about 80 percent of total administrative expenses. The GRA is reimbursed for the cost of administering the SDR Department through an assessment levied in proportion to each participant's allocation of SDRs. The GRA is also to be reimbursed for the expenses incurred in administering the PRGF Trust. However, following the establishment of the SRF and the consequent increase in net income, this reimbursement has been forgone and the amount that would otherwise have been reimbursed has been transferred to the PRGF-HIPC Trust. This arrangement has been in place since 1998 and is expected to continue up to 2004.

Borrowing

The IMF can borrow to supplement its quota resources. It maintains two standing borrowing arrangements with official lenders and can borrow from private markets, although it has not done so to date. Borrowing has played an important role in providing temporary, supplemental resources to the IMF at critical junctures in the past (Table II.7). In recent years, the borrowing arrangements with official lenders have been enlarged and their participation broadened, strengthening IMF liquidity.

---

[46] The basic (unadjusted) rate of remuneration has been equal to the SDR interest rate since February 1, 1987. However, refundable adjustments to that rate are made under "burden sharing." The Articles require that the rate of remuneration be maintained in the range of 80–100 percent of the SDR interest rate. The current relationship between the rate of remuneration and the SDR interest rate is governed by Rule I-10.

TABLE II.7. IMF BORROWING
(In billions of SDRs)

	Number of Countries or Central Banks	Agreed Amount
Current borrowing arrangements		
General Arrangements to Borrow (1983–2003)	11	17.0
Associated agreement with Saudi Arabia (1983–2003)	1	1.5
New Arrangements to Borrow (1998–2003)	25	34.0
Past borrowing arrangements		
General Arrangements to Borrow (1962–83)	10	6.4
Oil facility (1974)	7	2.8
Oil facility (1975)	12	2.9
Supplementary financing facility (1979–84)	14	7.8
Enlarged access to resources		
Medium-term (1981)		
Saudi Arabian Monetary Agency (SAMA)	1	8.0
Short-term (1981)		
Bank for International Settlements (BIS) and others	19	1.3
Short-term (1984)		
SAMA, BIS, Government of Japan, and National Bank of Belgium	4	6.0
Government of Japan (1986)	1	3.0

Current Borrowing Arrangements

The General Arrangements to Borrow have been in place since 1962. The GAB were originally conceived as arrangements whereby the main industrial (Group of Ten) countries agreed to stand ready to lend the IMF up to specified amounts of their currencies, thereby strengthening its financial position. These loans would be made when supplementary resources were needed by the IMF to help finance drawings by GAB participants in a setting where such financing would forestall or cope with an impairment of the international monetary system. Because the industrial countries have the largest quotas and may, when they need to, claim a large proportion of the IMF's usable resources, the GAB provide strong support for the IMF's financial soundness and for ensuring that resources available to other countries are not reduced.

The GAB enable the IMF to borrow specified amounts of currencies from 11 industrial countries or their central banks, under certain circumstances, at market-related rates of interest (Table II.8). The potential amount of credit available to the IMF under the GAB is SDR 17 billion, with an additional SDR 1.5 billion available under an associated agreement with Saudi Arabia.

The GAB are reviewed and renewed regularly. A broad review of the GAB was undertaken in 1983, at the outset of the developing country debt crisis. The most important changes to emerge from that review were the substantial enlargement of the GAB to its present size (from about SDR 6 billion), the addition of SDR 1.5 billion under the associated agreement with Saudi Arabia, and the change to permit use of the GAB to finance IMF lending to nonparticipants in the GAB if the IMF faces an inadequacy of resources. Since 1983, the GAB and the associated agreement with Saudi Arabia have been renewed every four or five years without further modification, most recently for a further five-year period from December 26, 1998.

The GAB have been activated ten times. The GAB were last activated in July 1998 for an amount of SDR 6.3 billion (SDR 1.4 billion of which was drawn) in connection with the financing of an Extended Arrangement for Russia. The activation for Russia was canceled in March 1999, when the IMF repaid the outstanding amount following the coming into effect of the Eleventh General Review of Quotas and payment of the bulk of the quota increases. Prior to the activation for Russia, the most recent activation occurred in 1977, when the IMF borrowed for lending to the United Kingdom and Italy under Stand-By Arrangements, and in 1978 to finance a reserve tranche purchase by the United States. A proposal for calls on the GAB by the IMF's Managing Director can become effective only if it is accepted by the GAB participants, and the proposal is then approved by the Executive Board.

The IMF also has New Arrangements to Borrow to deal with financial crises. Following the Mexican financial crisis in December 1994, concern that substantially more resources might be needed to respond to future financial crises prompted participants in the June 1995 Group of Seven Halifax Summit to call on the Group of Ten and other financially strong countries to develop financing arrangements that would double the amount available to the IMF under the GAB. The NAB became effective on November 17, 1998.

The NAB effectively double the resources available under the GAB. The NAB are a set of credit arrangements between the IMF and 25 members and institutions to provide supplementary resources to the IMF to forestall or cope with an impairment of the international monetary system or to deal with an exceptional situation to the stability of that system. The NAB do not

TABLE II.8. GENERAL AND NEW ARRANGEMENTS TO BORROW
(In millions of SDRs)

Participant	General Arrangements to Borrow	New Arrangements to Borrow
Australia	n.a.	810.0
Austria	n.a.	412.0
Belgium	595.0	967.0
Canada	892.5	1,396.0
Denmark	n.a.	371.0
Deutsche Bundesbank	2,380.0	3,557.0
Finland	n.a.	340.0
France	1,700.0	2,577.0
Hong Kong Monetary Authority	n.a.	340.0
Italy	1,105.0	1,772.0
Japan	2,125.0	3,557.0
Korea	n.a.	340.0
Kuwait	n.a.	345.0
Luxembourg	n.a.	340.0
Malaysia	n.a.	340.0
Netherlands	850.0	1,316.0
Norway	n.a.	383.0
Saudi Arabia	n.a.	1,780.0
Singapore	n.a.	340.0
Spain	n.a.	672.0
Sveriges Riksbank	382.5	859.0
Swiss National Bank	1,020.0	1,557.0
Thailand	n.a.	340.0
United Kingdom	1,700.0	2,577.0
United States	4,250.0	6,712.0
Total	17,000.0	34,000.0
Associated agreement with Saudi Arabia	1,500.0	n.a.

replace the GAB, which remain in force. However, the NAB are the first and principal recourse in the event of a need to provide supplementary resources to the IMF. The total amount of resources available to the IMF under the NAB and GAB combined is SDR 34 billion.

The NAB can be renewed and enlarged. The NAB decision will be in effect for five years from its effective date and may be renewed, at which time an IMF member or institution that is not currently a participant in the NAB may be accepted as a participant, if the IMF and participants representing 80 percent of the total credit arrangements agree to the request. New participants may be accepted at other times by way of an amendment to the NAB adopted by a decision of the IMF's Executive Board and with the concurrence of participants representing 85 percent of total credit arrangements. Commitments from participants are based on relative economic strength, as measured by actual IMF quotas, as a predominant criterion.

Activation procedures for the NAB are modeled on the GAB. The NAB have been activated once — to finance a Stand-By Arrangement for Brazil in December 1998, when the IMF called on funding of SDR 9.1 billion (SDR 2.9 billion of which was used). This activation was canceled on March 11, 1999, when the IMF repaid the outstanding amount following the entry into effect of the Eleventh General Review of Quotas and payment of the bulk of the quota increases.

Past Borrowing Arrangements

The IMF borrowed extensively when payments imbalances were large and persistent. Reliance on borrowing was especially heavy during the period of large payments imbalances between the early 1970s and the mid-1980s, when borrowing financed 40–60 percent of IMF credit. The need for supplemental resources to meet the heavy demand for IMF resources stemmed in part from the relatively small increases in quotas approved in the 1970s, and the need to bridge to the increases in quotas in 1980 and 1983. Also important was the skewed distribution of payments imbalances relative to the distribution of quotas at the time:

- large payments surpluses were concentrated in a comparatively small number of members with relatively small quotas; and
- payments deficits were far more widely dispersed and were large relative to the quotas of most members.

The IMF has borrowed only from official sources. Borrowing has been almost exclusively from members or their monetary authorities, the exceptions being nonmember Switzerland (now a member), the Hong Kong Monetary Authority (under the NAB), and the Bank for International Settlements (BIS). Borrowing from official sources has the advantage that these lenders are familiar with the IMF's needs and operational features, and there is by now a substantial body of experience from which to draw. The IMF is permitted to borrow from private sources and has considered this option on several occasions: the prevailing view has been that resort to private market borrowing would change the cooperative and monetary nature of the institution in ways that would be undesirable; a number of operational issues would also need to be addressed, such as the use of collateral, managing financial risk, and the cost relative to official borrowing.

Borrowing arrangements share many common characteristics:

- *Denomination of borrowing.* The indebtedness of members to the IMF is denominated in SDRs. To avoid exchange risks, IMF borrowing has generally been denominated in SDRs or the currencies that make up the SDR basket in proportion to their weight in that basket.
- *Media of payment.* The IMF cannot borrow SDRs. In most bilateral borrowing agreements, the lender has provided U.S. dollars or its own freely usable currency, or the lender has undertaken to convert its currency into a freely usable currency as needed by the IMF. For repayment, the IMF has generally sought maximum flexibility in the borrowing agreement but lenders have on occasion insisted on repayment in the currency of their choice, usually U.S. dollars or their own currency.
- *Maturities.* The IMF seeks to match the maturities of its assets and liabilities. Under the two Oil Facilities and the SFF, for example, the IMF borrowed when currency was needed for purchase and repaid lenders when the corresponding repurchases were made. This was not possible under the borrowing agreements established for the Enlarged Access Policy (EAP), as some central banks were willing to lend only at the short end of the maturity spectrum (see Table II.7). The resulting mismatch of maturities led to the establishment of Borrowed Resources Suspense Accounts within the GRA as a means of holding and investing temporarily currencies not yet needed to finance purchases under the EAP.
- *Liquidity and transferability.* Borrowing agreements with lenders other than the BIS have consistently provided for encashability at face value upon representation of balance of payments need. These agreements further stipulate that the IMF would give such a representation the overwhelming benefit of the doubt. A member's lending to the IMF is therefore regarded as a liquid reserve asset and is included as part of the member's international reserves. In addition, claims on the IMF are

normally transferable to other official holders, which provides some protection to the IMF's liquidity.

• *Interest rates.* In the early years of the IMF, interest rates on IMF borrowing and charges on purchases financed by borrowed resources were very low. Following the introduction of remuneration with the First Amendment of the Articles of Agreement in 1969, more attention was paid to the rate of return on the reserves that members made available to the IMF. Market rates were increasingly seen by members as the opportunity cost of lending to the IMF. In line with market practice, borrowing agreements since 1977 have provided for floating interest rates. To protect the IMF's income position, the cost of borrowing plus a small margin has been reflected in the rate of charge on the use of borrowed resources.

Management of Financial Resources and the Liquidity Position

As noted above, not all of the IMF's resources are immediately available for lending. The IMF's usable resources consist of currencies of IMF members with a strong balance of payments position and SDRs, which stem mainly from quota payments. The institution maintains substantial holdings of gold and other fixed assets, but these are not used in lending operations. Borrowing by the IMF to finance the extension of credit through the GRA is an important complement to the use of its quota resources but remains the exception rather than the rule. Borrowing is, however, a central feature of IMF lending under the PRGF, as discussed in Chapter IV.

The usability of the IMF's currency holdings varies over time. In principle, the currencies of all members are available for use in IMF transactions. Members have an obligation to convert balances of their currency purchased from the IMF by other members into one of the four freely usable currencies: the U.S. dollar, the euro, the Japanese yen, and the pound sterling.[47] The IMF determines which members are in a sufficiently strong external position to meet this currency exchange obligation when drawing up its quarterly financial transactions plan (see below). The currencies of these

---

[47]Article V, Section 3*(e)*(i).

members are considered to be usable in IMF transactions for the duration of
that quarter, while all other currencies are considered unusable.

The IMF's holdings of SDRs are a readily usable resource, but these holdings account for only a small fraction of the IMF's assets. The use of SDRs
held by the IMF is therefore not limited to the same extent as the use of its
currency holdings. The IMF periodically establishes a long-term target range
for the level of its SDR holdings, which guides the actual use of SDRs in
IMF transactions. Other factors affecting the level of the IMF's holdings of
SDRs are discussed in Chapter III.

The IMF closely monitors its liquidity position. Table II.9 presents the
IMF's financial resources and liquidity position as of April 30, 2001.[48] For
this purpose, the stock of usable resources is adjusted downward to take into
account amounts already committed to members under existing IMF
arrangements. A further downward adjustment is made to ensure that the
IMF retains at all times sufficient working balances of each of the currencies
of members included in the financial transactions plan. The resulting
amount of net uncommitted usable resources is in principle available to
meet new demand for IMF resources. In practice, however, the adequacy of
the IMF's liquidity position must also take into account the existence of liquid claims accumulated by its creditor members: reserve tranche positions
and any outstanding loans under the GAB and NAB. These are considered
liquid liabilities because they can be drawn at short notice in the event of
balance of payments need, akin to demand deposits in a commercial bank,
and are thus the first claim on IMF resources. The liquidity ratio ties these
two concepts together in a single measure of the IMF's liquidity. Historically,
the liquidity ratio has never fallen below 25–30 percent.

Financial Transactions Plan

The IMF manages its usable resources through a financial transactions
plan. This is the mechanism through which the IMF selects the members
whose currencies are to be used in IMF transactions and allocates the
financing of those transactions among members included in the plan. Both
currencies and SDRs are included in the financial transactions plan for
transfers (credits) from the IMF to borrowing members but only currencies

---

[48]The IMF's "Financial Resources and Liquidity Position" is posted monthly on the
IMF's website (http://www.imf.org/external/np/tre/liquid).

TABLE II.9. IMF FINANCIAL RESOURCES AND LIQUIDITY POSITION,
APRIL 30, 2001
(In billions of SDRs unless otherwise indicated)

I.	Total resources	217.5
	Members' currencies	207.9
	Gold holdings	5.9
	SDR holdings	2.4
	Other assets	1.3
	Available under GAB/NAB activation	—
II.	Unusable resources	105.4
III.	Usable resources (I – II)	112.1
IV.	Amounts committed under arrangements	18.1
V.	Minimum working balances	15.3
VI.	Net uncommitted usable resources (III – IV – V)	78.7
VII.	Balances available under the GAB/NAB	34.0
VIII.	Liquid liabilities	46.7
	Reserve tranche positions	46.7
	Outstanding borrowing under the GAB/NAB	—
IX.	Liquidity ratio (VI/VIII, in percent)	168.4

Note: Numbers may not add to totals due to rounding.

are included for receipts (repayments) from borrowing members; receipts in
SDRs are not managed through the plan as the IMF has little or no discretion over their use by members. The total amount for transfers in the transactions plan is based on the expected volume of credit to be extended to
members and operational payments by the IMF (such as interest on official
borrowing by the IMF) during the plan period. Receipts in currencies are
estimated on the basis of the schedule of forthcoming repayments and the
preferences of members with respect to the media of payment (i.e., currencies versus SDRs).

Currency selection is based on judgments about the external positions of members. The currencies of members are selected for inclusion in the financial transactions plan based on a finding by the IMF that the member's balance of payments and reserve position is sufficiently strong. Specific indicators of external strength are used to maintain a reasonable degree of consistency among members, but the assessment of a member's combined balance of payments and reserve position is ultimately a matter of judgment. It has not therefore been considered desirable to rely on automatic indicators or to define rigidly the notion of a sufficiently strong external position; the circumstances of members, including their need to hold reserves, differ considerably.

All relevant factors and data are considered in this assessment. Particular emphasis is placed on recent and prospective current account balances, external competitiveness, and external debt indicators, especially those offering insights into the member's exposure to short-term liquidity strains. Members may be included in the financial transactions plan even though there may be some elements of weakness in their overall balance of payments and reserve position.

Two broader considerations underlying the financial structure of the IMF have guided the staff and the Executive Board in coming to conclusions about a member's external strength for the purpose of participation in the financial transactions plan.

- First, the IMF draws on a wide range of members—large and small, advanced, developing, and transition—for its financial activities, reflecting first and foremost the cooperative nature of the institution. Broad participation of members in the financial transactions plan also works to maximize the liquidity of the GRA.
- Second, the use of a member's currency in the financial transactions plan generally entails a change in the composition of the member's international reserves. For most of these members, IMF transactions involve a reduction (increase) in their foreign exchange holdings, which is fully offset by an increase (decrease) in their reserve tranche position in the IMF. This creditor position is included as part of the member's international reserves as it is a liquid claim on foreign exchange resources that can be drawn on demand in the event of balance of payments need.

Decisions on the selection of currencies are taken by the Executive Board. The staff proposes a list of members it considers sufficiently strong each quarter, and the Executive Board takes a decision based on this list. It is open to an Executive Director to request the exclusion or inclusion of any member, but the decision rests with the Executive Board as a whole. A member's consent to its inclusion is not required, although its views on its balance of payments and reserve position are taken into account by the Executive Board before a decision is taken. The outcome of the financial transactions plan is published on the IMF's website.[49]

Currency allocation aims to maintain broadly even participation among members. The allocation of transfers and receipts among members in the financial transactions plan is based on guidelines established by the Executive Board.[50] The currencies of all members included in the financial transactions plan are allocated for transfers in direct proportion to their quotas. Receipts are allocated to members' currencies included in the plan so as to ensure that the creditor positions of members included in the plan remain broadly balanced over time in relation to quota. The net impact of both transfers and receipts on reserve tranche positions is illustrated in Figure II.6.

If a currency included in the financial transactions plan is not one of the currencies that the IMF has determined to be freely usable in the principal foreign exchange markets, the issuing member is required, if requested by a purchasing member at the time of the purchase, to exchange the amount of its currency sold by the IMF for a freely usable currency (in most cases, the U.S. dollar) at the representative exchange rate as advised by the IMF. Procedures have also been established for the exchange of each freely usable currency into other freely usable currencies. Similar procedures apply to exchanges of currencies related to repurchases.

Special Disbursement Account

The SDA was initially activated to receive transfers from the Trust Fund. The Trust Fund had been funded largely from the sale of gold and upon its termination in 1981, all Trust Fund loan repayments were transferred to the SDA. Loans were provided from the SDA under the Structural Adjustment Facility (SAF), which was established in March 1986 to provide balance of

---

[49]The "Quarterly Report on Financing IMF Transactions" is posted one quarter after the end of the period on the IMF's website (http://www.imf.org/external/np/tre/ftp).

[50]See *Selected Decisions and Documents of the International Monetary Fund* (Washington: IMF, Twenty-Fifth Issue, June 30, 2000), pp. 260–65.

FIGURE II.6. RESERVE POSITIONS, AS OF APRIL 30, 2001

(In percent of quota)

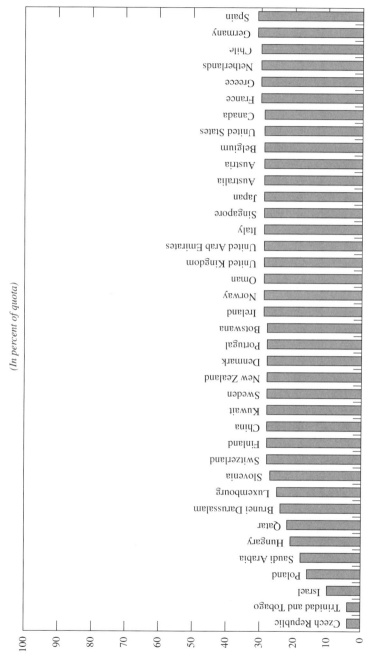

Source: International Monetary Fund, *International Financial Statistics.*

payments assistance on concessional terms to qualifying low-income member countries, from 1986 until the end of 1995, when the SAF itself was phased out.[51] From the establishment of the Enhanced Structural Adjustment Facility (ESAF) in December 1987 until February 1994, unused SDA resources were also used to finance ESAF loans.

The assets of the SDA now consist of the remaining loan balances outstanding under the SAF and investments in marketable fixed-income securities. These assets originate from the transfers received from the Trust Fund and the profits from the sale of a portion of the IMF's gold in financial year 2000. The net income from the investment of gold profits has been authorized for transfers, on an as-needed basis in accordance with the decisions of the IMF, to the Poverty Reduction and Growth Facility–Heavily Indebted Poor Countries Trust (PRGF-HIPC Trust).

Chapter IV discusses the financing and conduct of concessional lending by the IMF, including the investment of SDA resources.

IMF Accounts in Member Countries

The IMF conducts its financial dealings with a member through the fiscal agency and the depository designated by the member. The fiscal agency may be the member's treasury (ministry of finance), central bank, official monetary agency, stabilization fund, or other similar agency. The IMF can only deal with, or through, the designated fiscal agency, which is authorized to carry out transactions with the IMF on behalf of the member country. In addition, each member is required to designate its central bank as a depository for the IMF's holdings of the member's currency, or if it has no central bank, a monetary agency or a commercial bank acceptable to the IMF. Most members of the IMF have designated their central bank as both the depository and the fiscal agency. The depository is required to pay out of the IMF's holdings of the member's currency, on demand and without delay, sums to any payee named by the IMF in the member's own territory, and to hold securities on behalf of the IMF should the member decide to issue nonnegotiable, non-interest-bearing notes, or similar instruments, in substitution for part of the IMF's currency holdings. Each member guarantees all assets of the IMF against loss resulting from failure or default on the part of the

---

[51]Interest on SAF loans is charged at ½ of 1 percent a year.

depository. Thus, the IMF's pool of currencies and reserve assets in the GRA are not held at the IMF, but in depositories in the member countries.

The depository maintains, without any service charge or commission, two accounts that are used to record the IMF's holdings of the member's currency: the IMF No. 1 Account and the IMF No. 2 Account. The No. 1 Account is used for IMF transactions, including subscription payments, purchases and repurchases (i.e., use and repayment of GRA resources), and repayment of resources borrowed by the IMF. Payment of charges on the use of IMF credit and the IMF's payment of interest on reserve tranche positions are conducted in SDRs and therefore not recorded in these accounts. Provided that a minimum is maintained in the No. 1 Account, as explained below, all these transactions can alternatively be carried out through the IMF Securities Account. A member may establish an IMF Securities Account in order to substitute parts of the holdings in the IMF No. 1 Account with nonnegotiable, non-interest-bearing notes, or similar instruments payable to the IMF on demand when the currency is needed for the IMF's transactions. The depository holds these notes for safekeeping and acts as the agent of the IMF to obtain encashment of the notes in order to maintain, at all times, the minimum required balance in the No. 1 Account.[52]

The No. 2 Account is used for the IMF's administrative expenditures and receipts (for example, from sales of IMF publications) in the member's currency and within its territory. The balances in both the No. 1 and No. 2 Accounts that originate from the payment of the local currency portion of quota subscriptions do not yield any interest for the IMF. The currency portion of the subscribed capital, while fully paid, is held in non-interest-bearing form and generates no income for the IMF until used and converted into claims on members in the form of use of IMF credit.

Disclosure of Financial Position with the IMF in the Member Country[53]

When a member has designated the central bank as both depository and fiscal agent, the central bank should present the full financial position of the

---

[52]If any payment by the IMF reduces the balance in the No. 1 Account below a minimum of ¼ of 1 percent of the member's quota, the balance is to be restored to that level by the next business day through the encashment of sufficient notes.

[53]This discussion presents IMF member positions in the General and SDR Departments.

member with the IMF in its balance sheet.[54] A central bank may choose to indicate this on either a gross or net basis. The position in the General Department is presented on a gross basis if the IMF No. 1, No. 2, and Securities Accounts are shown as liabilities and the member's quota is shown as an asset. Membership in the SDR Department would be indicated by showing SDR holdings as an asset and the cumulative SDR allocation as a liability.

Members may also choose to reflect their financial position on a net basis. A member who has a net reserve tranche position in the IMF and is not using IMF credit would present the net reserve tranche position as an asset.[55] Members with a net reserve tranche position who are also using credit in the GRA would disclose the reserve tranche as an asset and currency holdings stemming from the use of IMF credit as a liability, since the IMF is not entitled to demand settlement or offset a member's use of credit from its reserve tranche position. The members' position in the SDR Department may also be shown on a net basis. The presentation of IMF-related assets and liabilities should be further elaborated in the explanatory notes to the financial statements and, as a minimum, provide information not available in the balance sheet regarding the member's quota, the composition of the IMF's currency holdings, and the maturity structure of IMF credit, if any.

In cases where the central bank acts as depository and the ministry of finance, treasury, or a similar agency is the fiscal agent, it is recommended that the central bank record all IMF-related assets and liabilities and offset these against government accounts.[56] While practices may differ depending on the relationship between the central bank and the agency acting as fiscal agent, this approach ensures public disclosure of the member's financial relationship with the IMF, since government agencies typically do not pre-

---

[54]For this reason it is also recommended to include the Securities Account in the IMF position, even though the actual securities may be issued by the government. The IMF considers securities issued in lieu of currency deposits to the IMF No. 1 Account equivalent to currency holdings because they are encashable on demand. Exclusion of the Securities Account would therefore misrepresent the member's overall IMF position.

[55]A member has a net reserve tranche position when its quota exceeds the IMF's holdings of its currencies, excluding currencies stemming from the use of IMF credit and holdings in the No. 2 Account that are less than $\frac{1}{10}$ of 1 percent of quota.

[56]Of the IMF's 183 member countries, only 41 have not designated their central bank as the fiscal agent.

pare financial statements.[57] Consolidating the IMF position in the balance sheet of the central bank also allows for a simple reconciliation between foreign reserves data monitored under an IMF-supported program or published by a member and the balance sheet of the central bank. Since most central banks are subject to an annual audit, full inclusion of the IMF position provides additional assurance about the accuracy and availability of foreign reserves.

Appendix IV illustrates how IMF membership could be presented on either a gross or net basis in the balance sheet of a central bank that acts as both fiscal agent and depository for the member with the IMF.

---

[57]PRGF transactions would also be shown in the balance sheet of the central bank if the central bank were the recipient of the proceeds of PRGF disbursements.

III

SDR Department

The SDR Department was established to conduct all transactions in SDRs, following the creation of the new international reserve asset by the IMF in 1969. The Articles require that the General and SDR Departments be kept strictly separate, such that assets in one department cannot be used to meet liabilities of the other, except for the reimbursement of the General Department for the expenses incurred in conducting the business of the SDR Department.[1] This separation reflects the fact that the SDR facility is an entirely separate financial mechanism within the IMF. A member of the IMF need not be a member of the SDR Department, though currently all are.

The SDR itself is an international reserve asset created by the IMF to supplement other reserve assets whose growth was inadequate to finance the expansion of international trade and finance under the Bretton Woods system in the postwar period. The SDR is not a currency, nor is it a claim on the IMF. Rather, it is potentially a claim on the freely usable currencies of IMF members.

The SDR's value as a reserve asset derives from the commitments of members to hold and accept SDRs and to honor various obligations connected with the proper operation of the SDR system. The IMF ensures the SDR's claim on freely usable currencies in two ways: by designating IMF members with a strong external position to purchase SDRs from members with weak external positions, and through arrangement of voluntary exchanges between participants in a managed market. Thus, the functioning of the SDR Department, like that of the General Department, is based on the principle of mutuality and intergovernmental cooperation.

The value of the SDR and its yield, or interest rate, are not determined by supply and demand in a market, but are set by the IMF. They have been defined in terms of the prevailing exchange rate system in effect, in the early

---

[1]The IMF levies an assessment on each participant (in proportion to its cumulative SDR allocations) at the end of each financial year to cover the expenses of conducting the business of the SDR Department. The rate of assessment is generally very small; for the financial year ended April 30, 2001, it was 0.011198 percent of cumulative allocations (see Appendix I).

years being fixed under the Bretton Woods fixed exchange rate system and later as a value of and interest on a basket of currencies under the floating exchange rate regime. Currently, the SDR's value is calculated daily using a basket of four major currencies: the euro, Japanese yen, pound sterling, and U.S. dollar. The SDR interest rate was initially set at a low fixed level, but now is calculated weekly using market yields on short-term government securities denominated in the currencies in the SDR basket, except for the euro area where the Euro Interbank Offered Rate (Euribor) is now used in the absence of a short-term public sector security that is representative of the entire euro area. While both the valuation and yield of the SDR are linked to the prevailing markets of their component exchange and interest rates, there is no market for the SDR itself where excess supply or demand pressures can be eliminated by adjustments in the price, or value, of the asset. Rather, the IMF itself manages the flows of SDRs to ensure liquidity in the system.

Under certain conditions, the IMF may allocate SDRs to members participating in the SDR Department in proportion to their IMF quotas at the time by approval of 85 percent of the voting power of the IMF. Decisions to allocate SDRs have been reached only twice; a third, special "equity" allocation, is pending ratification. As SDRs accounted for less than 1½ percent of members' nongold reserves at end-April 2001, their role as a reserve asset has been quite limited.

The SDR is a purely official asset and can only be held and used by member country participants in the SDR Department, the IMF, and certain designated official entities. The SDR is used almost exclusively in transactions with the IMF and it serves as the unit of account of the IMF and a number of other international organizations. Efforts to promote its use in private markets have been largely ineffective.

Since the rate of interest paid by members using SDRs is the same as the rate of interest earned by members holding SDRs, the interest payments and receipts cancel out overall, so that net income in the SDR Department is always zero, as illustrated in the financial statements of the department.

In 1996, the IMF sponsored a seminar on the future of the SDR which concluded that the SDR was unlikely to become established as the principal reserve asset of the international monetary system in the near future in view of the globalization of private financial markets. However, there was considerable sentiment in favor of maintaining at least the present role of the SDR.

The remainder of the chapter expands upon these points by first explaining when, why, and how the SDR was created. This is followed by a description of the key characteristics of the SDR as a reserve asset, including the methods used to value the SDR and determine its yield. Next, the rules for allocating, holding, and using SDRs are discussed.

Most of the balance of the chapter deals with the operation of the SDR system as it functions in the official sector. The circular flow of SDRs among holders is described, highlighting the key role played by the IMF and the development of a managed market for SDRs among a number of relatively large holders with standing two-way (buying and selling) arrangements. The historical pattern of SDR holdings among debtors, creditors, and the IMF is shown, revealing persistent use of SDRs by IMF debtors, continuing large holdings of SDRs among a few IMF creditors, and periodic spikes in the flows of SDRs into the IMF resulting from the reserve asset payments associated with general quota increases. These developments underlie the need for the IMF to actively manage the circulation of SDRs through the quarterly financial transactions plan in order to maintain the system's liquidity.

The chapter concludes by showing how the previous discussion is reflected in the balance sheet and income statement of the SDR Department and by reporting on the outcome of an IMF seminar on "The Future of the SDR."

Background and Characteristics of the SDR

Creation of the SDR[2]

Gold was the central reserve asset of the international monetary system created at the Bretton Woods conference in 1944. Under the Bretton Woods system, the value of each currency was expressed in terms of gold (its par value) and member states were obliged to keep the exchange rates for their currencies within 1 percent of parity. In practice, most countries fulfilled this obligation by observing the par value against the U.S. dollar and by buying

---

[2]This section and the next rely on several papers in *The Future of the SDR in Light of Changes in the International Financial System*, ed. by Michael Mussa, James M. Boughton, and Peter Isard (Washington: International Monetary Fund, 1996), particularly the papers by Robert Solomon, "Creation and Evolution of the SDR"; Michael Mussa, "The Rationale for SDR Allocation Under the Present Articles of Agreement of the International Monetary Fund"; and K. Alec Chrystal, "The SDR and Its Characteristics as an Asset: An Appraisal," as well as "Evolution of the SDR: Paper Gold or Paper Tiger?" in James M. Boughton, *Silent Revolution: The International Monetary Fund, 1979–1989* (Washington: International Monetary Fund, 2001). See these sources for a more complete discussion of the issues addressed.

and selling their currencies for U.S. dollars, while the United States undertook to buy and sell gold freely for U.S. dollars at $35 a fine ounce, the par value of the U.S. dollar. This was also the "official price" of gold, at which all IMF transactions in gold were conducted.

In the early postwar years, the United States held about 60 percent of the world's official gold reserves and there was widespread concern over a "dollar shortage" as war-devastated countries sought to buy goods from the United States. Large capital outflows from the United States, exceeding its current account surplus, made it possible for these needs to be met. This net transfer of gold and dollars to the rest of the world helped other countries rebuild their reserves after the war. As the decade of the 1950s progressed, the dollar shortage ended and the European countries made their currencies convertible. By the late 1950s, the dollar shortage was replaced by what some observers called a "dollar glut," and in the 1960s an increasing number of countries sought to exchange dollars for gold from the United States, reflecting their fear that dollars were no longer "as good as gold."

It has been argued that the Bretton Woods par value system had an inherent flaw, the so-called Triffin Dilemma.[3] As long as the U.S. dollar was the primary foreign exchange reserve asset, a growing level of world trade and finance required a growing supply of dollars. That growing stock of dollars, however, required a persistent deficit in the U.S. balance of payments and this itself was a threat to the value of the dollar. Official holders of dollars became concerned that the relative value of their reserve assets might decrease in relation to the value of gold.

The other possible source of reserve growth in the system was through rising gold production. While gold initially provided more than three-fourths of global reserve increases after the war, this share had dropped to one-fourth in the first half of the 1960s and subsequently became negative. The dwindling supply of gold and poor outlook for increased production put pressure on the official price of gold which the United States and the larger European countries maintained through intervention in the London gold market. By 1968, these countries' central banks announced that they would no longer intervene in the private gold market. This led to the segmentation of the market for gold into two tiers — an official market where transactions

---

[3]Robert Triffin, *Gold and the Dollar Crisis: The Future of Convertibility* (New Haven: Yale University Press, rev. ed., 1961).

were undertaken at the official price, and a private market where rising prices were determined by supply and demand.

The solution to the problem of inadequate reserve growth in the system lay in creating an international reserve asset to supplement dollars and gold in official reserve holdings. Some countries favored the creation of a new reserve unit, while the United States, out of concern that such a unit would be a competitor for the dollar, preferred to build on the existing automatic drawing rights (the gold tranche) in the IMF. Thus, a scheme was debated in the mid-1960s by the Group of Ten ministers to create "reserve drawing rights" in the IMF, but some European countries feared this mechanism could be interpreted as a replacement for gold and suggested instead "special" drawing rights, and the name stuck. A blueprint for the creation of a new international reserve asset, the SDR, in amounts necessary to supplement supplies of gold and foreign exchange reserves was agreed at the Rio de Janeiro meeting of the IMF Board of Governors in September 1967, and SDRs were first allocated by the IMF in 1970.

At the time the SDR system was agreed, it was thought that for the first time the total stock of international reserves and its rate of growth would reflect deliberate international decisions rather than being determined solely by the accumulation of balances in reserve currencies and gold. Thus, it was envisaged that the IMF would become a major source of supply of both conditional liquidity through its traditional means of providing financial assistance, and of unconditional liquidity through the functioning of the SDR system. These views were subsequently reflected in the Second Amendment to the Articles of Agreement in 1978, which established that the obligation of members to collaborate regarding policies on reserve assets should be consistent with the objectives of promoting better international surveillance of international liquidity and making the SDR the principal reserve asset.

SDR as a Reserve Asset

The SDR has value and usefulness as a reserve asset because holdings in the IMF's SDR Department can be exchanged with other participants for national currencies. Note that SDRs are not liabilities of the IMF. Participants with a balance of payments need may use SDRs to acquire foreign exchange in a transaction by designation — that is, one in which another participant, designated by the IMF because of its strong balance of payments and reserve position, provides a freely usable currency in exchange for

SDRs (Box III.1). Provision of such foreign exchange is an obligation of participation in the SDR Department. A participant's obligation to provide currency, however, is limited to twice its cumulative allocation of SDRs, unless both the member and the IMF agree on a higher limit.

The designation mechanism guarantees that a participant with a need to use SDRs for balance of payments purposes is able to obtain the requisite freely usable currency without delay. This mechanism constitutes the legal backing of the SDR system and demonstrates its cooperative basis. In its operation, the SDR designation procedure works very much like the currency exchange system in the General Department. Since September 1987, however, no transactions by designation have taken place because all exchanges of SDRs for currency have been accommodated through voluntary transactions by agreement, which are discussed below in the section "System of Two-Way Arrangements." The IMF, however, continues to prepare a designation plan each quarter, tied to the quarterly financial transactions plan, on a contingency basis and as added insurance for the liquidity of the SDR financing mechanism.

An allocation of SDRs by the IMF provides each recipient, a participating member country, with a costless asset on which the holder neither earns nor pays interest.[4] Countries holding SDRs can use these assets by exchanging them for freely usable currencies at a value determined by the value of the SDR basket. Countries using their SDRs necessarily hold fewer SDRs than they had been allocated, and they pay interest at the SDR interest rate on the difference between their cumulative allocations and their current holdings of SDRs. Other countries are effectively net creditors in the SDR system by holding more SDRs than their cumulative allocations, and they receive a corresponding amount of interest on their holdings of SDRs in excess of their cumulative allocations.

Valuing the SDR and Determining the SDR Interest Rate

The SDR was initially defined as equivalent to 0.888671 grams of fine gold. As this was the par value of the U.S. dollar under the Bretton Woods system, the SDR was also equivalent to one U.S. dollar. This outcome satisfied both camps in the negotiations that lead to the creation of the new international

---

[4]Technically, the recipient earns interest on its holdings and pays interest on its cumulative allocations, but the two interest rates are identical and the payments therefore net out as long as a recipient simply holds its cumulative allocation of SDRs.

BOX III.1. THE DESIGNATION MECHANISM

Article XIX of the IMF's Articles of Agreement provides for a designation mechanism that underpins the usability of the SDR. Participation in the SDR Department entails the obligation to provide usable currencies in exchange for SDRs when designated, and accords the right to use SDRs in case of a balance of payments need.

Under the designation mechanism, the IMF designates certain participants, whose external positions are deemed sufficiently strong, to receive specified amounts of SDRs from other participants and, in exchange, to provide the latter with equivalent amounts of freely usable currencies (i.e., U.S. dollars, euros, Japanese yen, and pounds sterling). The designation mechanism ensures that, in case of need, participants can use SDRs to obtain foreign currency reserves at short notice.[1]

Quarterly designation plans, approved by the Executive Board, list participants subject to designation and set the maximum limits to the amounts of SDRs that can be designated to each. There are three basic criteria for designation:

• Participants are subject to designation only if their balance of payments and gross reserve positions are considered "sufficiently strong."

• The Executive Board determines the amounts of designation for individual participants in such a manner as to promote, over time, harmonization (or equalization) of the "excess holdings ratios" of participants.[2]

• A participant's obligation to provide currency against SDRs in designation is limited to the point at which its SDR holdings in excess of its cumulative allocation are twice its cumulative allocation of SDRs, unless the designee and the IMF agree on a higher limit.

---

[1]A participant wishing to sell its SDRs in transactions with designation is required to make a representation to the IMF that it has a need to use its SDRs because of its balance of payments position or developments in its reserves, and not for the sole purpose of changing the composition of its reserves (Article XIX, Section 3(a)).

[2]The excess holdings ratio is calculated as the member's actual SDR holdings minus its cumulative allocation as a percent of its quota.

---

reserve asset—those who sought a replacement for gold and those who sought a replacement for the U.S. dollar. When the dollar was devalued against gold in 1971, the SDR retained its nominal gold value and was termed "paper gold." In keeping with the SDR's character as paper gold, the interest rate on the SDR was initially fixed at the relatively low level of 1.5 percent a year.

With the final collapse of the Bretton Woods par value system in 1973, most major countries adopted floating exchange rate regimes. As gold no longer played a central role as the anchor of the international monetary system, the rationale for defining the SDR in terms of gold was weakened, and in 1974 the SDR was redefined as a basket of currencies. Initially, the currencies of the 16 IMF members with at least 1 percent of world trade were included in the basket. At the same time, the interest rate on the SDR was raised to 5 percent, consistent with a new policy of setting the rate semiannually at about half of the level of a combined market interest rate which was defined as a weighted average of interest rates on short-term market instruments in France, Germany, Japan, the United States, and the United Kingdom.

The 16-currency SDR basket provided a poor unit of account because it was difficult and costly to replicate and it included some currencies that were not widely traded. It was a poor store of value because it had a lower yield than substitute reserve assets. As a result of these shortcomings, in 1981 the valuation of the SDR was simplified to the same five-currency basket on which the SDR interest rate was based, while the interest rate itself was raised to 100 percent of market rates. Formally, the selection criterion for inclusion in the valuation basket was changed to the currencies of the five member countries with the largest exports of goods and services over the previous five years. These changes resulted in a unification of the SDR valuation and interest rate baskets composed of the five freely usable currencies recognized by the IMF: the U.S. dollar, the Japanese yen, the deutsche mark, the French franc, and the pound sterling. The currencies that determine the value of the SDR, the amount of each of these currencies in the basket, and the financial instruments used in determining the interest rate, are reviewed every five years.

The five-currency basket was simple enough to be readily replicable by financial markets while still ensuring that the value of the SDR would be fairly stable in the face of wide swings in exchange rates. The increase in the yield on the SDR made it more attractive to hold compared with other reserve assets and thereby increased creditor incentives to finance the IMF as the rate of remuneration was linked to the interest rate on the SDR. With the introduction of the euro in 1999, the deutsche mark and French franc in the SDR basket were replaced with equivalent amounts of euro, without changing the relative weight of the continental European currencies in the basket.

Current Method of SDR Valuation

The most recent revision of the SDR basket took place on January 1, 2001. The adoption of the euro as the common currency for several member states of the European Union necessitated a change in the criteria for selecting currencies for inclusion in the SDR valuation basket. In particular, the previous criterion was extended to include exports by a monetary union that includes IMF members. In the case of monetary unions, exports of goods and services exclude trade among members of the union.

A second selection criterion was also introduced to ensure that the currencies included in the SDR valuation basket are among the most widely used in international transactions. For this purpose, the IMF formalized the requirement that a currency selected for inclusion in the basket be "freely usable" in accordance with the criteria specified in Article XXX(f) of the IMF's Articles. Under this provision, a currency is "freely usable" if the Executive Board determines that it is, in fact, widely used to make payments for international transactions and is widely traded in the principal foreign exchange markets. The weights assigned to the currencies in the SDR basket continue to be based on the value of the exports of goods and services and the amount of reserves denominated in the respective currencies that are held by other members of the IMF over the previous five years.[5]

Four currencies met both selection criteria for inclusion in the SDR valuation basket and were assigned the weights shown in Table III.1, based on their roles in international trade and finance.

The amounts of each of the four currencies included in the new SDR valuation basket were calculated on December 29, 2000 in accordance with the new weights. The calculation was made on the basis of the average exchange rates for these currencies over the three months ending on that date in such a manner as to ensure that the value of the SDR was the same on December 29, 2000 under both the old and new valuation baskets.

The value of the SDR in terms of the U.S. dollar is calculated daily by the IMF as the sum of the market values in terms of the U.S. dollar of the amounts of each of the five currencies in the valuation basket. The actual, or effective, share of each currency in the valuation of the SDR on any particu-

---

[5]As the euro had been in existence for less than two years when the 2000 review of the SDR basket was undertaken, reserve holdings at end-1999 were used.

TABLE III.1. CURRENCY WEIGHTS IN SDR BASKET, 1996 AND 2001

(In percent)

Currency	Effective January 1, 2001	Previous Revision January 1, 1996
U.S. dollar	45	39
Euro[1]	29	
Deutsche mark		21
French franc		11
Japanese yen	15	18
Pound sterling	11	11

[1]On January 1, 1999, the deutsche mark and French franc in the SDR basket were replaced by equivalent amounts of euro.

lar day depends on the exchange rates prevailing on that day. An example of the valuation of the SDR is shown in Box III.2. The actual shares of currencies in the basket over the past decade are shown in Figure III.1. The valuation of the SDR is posted each morning, Washington time, on the IMF's website.[6]

Current Method of Determining the SDR Interest Rate

In 2000, the IMF also reviewed the method for determining the SDR interest rate and decided to continue to set the weekly interest rate on the basis of a weighted average of interest rates on short-term instruments in the markets of the currencies included in the SDR valuation basket. However, it changed the financial instruments used as the representative interest rates for the euro and Japanese yen.

The representative interest rate for the Japanese yen was changed from the three-month rate on certificates of deposit to the yield on Japanese Government 13-week financing bills. In keeping with the shift to a currency-based system of SDR valuation, the representative rate for the euro, the three-month Euribor, replaced the national financial instruments of France and Germany. The interest rate on the three-month U.S. and U.K. Treasury

---

[6]See http://www.imf.org/external/np/tre/sdr/basket.htm.

Box III.2. SDR Valuation: Determination of Currency Amounts and Actual Daily Weights

Currency amounts are calculated on the last business day preceding the date the new basket becomes effective. On that day, currency amounts are derived from the weights decided by the Executive Board using the average exchange rate for each currency over the preceding three months. Currency amounts are adjusted proportionally to ensure that the value of the SDR is the same before and after the revision.

The currency amounts remain fixed for the subsequent five-year period. As a result, the actual weight of each currency in the value of the SDR changes on a daily basis as a result of changes in exchange rates.

April 30, 2001

Currency	Initial Weight Decided in 2000	Currency Amount Under Rule O-1	Exchange Rate[1] April 30, 2001	U.S. Dollar Equivalent	Actual Weight April 30, 2001
Euro	29	0.4260	0.8871	0.377905	30
Japanese yen	15	21.0000	123.53	0.169999	13
Pounds sterling	11	0.0984	1.4318	0.140889	11
U. S. dollars	45	0.5770	1.0000	0.577000	46
				1.265793	100
US$1 = SDR				0.790019[2]	
SDR 1 = US$				1.26579[3]	

[1]The exchange rate for the Japanese yen is expressed in terms of currency units per U.S. dollar; other rates are expressed as U.S. dollars per currency unit.

[2]IMF Rule O-2(a) defines the value of the U.S. dollar in terms of the SDR as the reciprocal of the sum of the equivalents in U.S. dollars of the amounts of the currencies in the SDR basket, calculated on the basis of exchange rate quotations at noon in the London market, rounded to six significant digits. If the London market is closed, quotations are taken from the New York market; if both of these markets are closed, reference rates of the European Central Bank are used.

[3]The reciprocal of the value of the U.S. dollar in terms of the SDR, rounded to six significant digits.

FIGURE III.1. ACTUAL CURRENCY WEIGHTS IN SDR BASKET, JULY 1990–APRIL 2001

(In percent; end of period)[1]

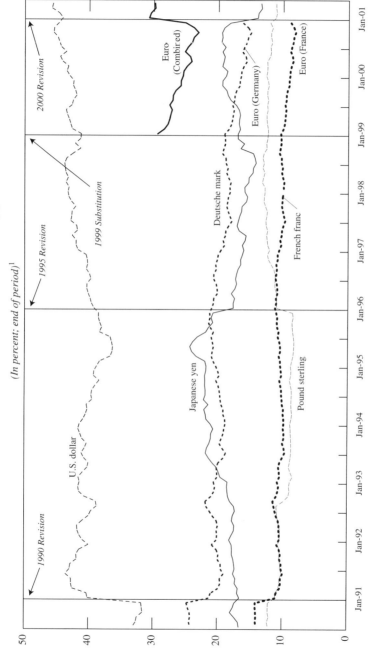

[1]Except for January 1, 1991, 1996, 1999, and 2001.

bills continue to serve as the representative interest rates for the U.S. dollar and pound sterling, respectively.

The SDR interest rate is calculated weekly by the IMF as the sum of the yields on the respective financial instruments in the basket, in terms of SDRs, using the currency amounts in the valuation basket as weights. Thus, the effective weights of the financial instruments representing each component currency reflect the level of interest rates in each currency as well as the level of exchange rates and the currency amounts in the basket (Box III.3). As a result, these weights differ from the effective weights of the same currencies in the SDR valuation basket, which reflect only the level of exchange rates and the currency amounts in the basket. For example, the weight of the Japanese yen in the interest rate basket is much lower than in the valuation basket, reflecting Japan's currently low interest rates. The SDR interest rate for the current week is posted on Monday morning, Washington time, on the IMF's website.[7]

Allocations and Cancellations of SDRs

The IMF has the authority (Article XV, Section 1, and Article XVIII) to create unconditional liquidity through general allocations of SDRs to participants in the SDR Department in proportion to their quotas in the IMF. The IMF cannot allocate SDRs to itself or to other holders it prescribes. The Articles also provide for the cancellation of SDRs, although to date there have been no cancellations. In its decisions on general allocations of SDRs, the IMF, as prescribed under its Articles, has sought to meet the long-term global need to supplement existing reserve assets, while promoting the attainment of the IMF's purposes and avoiding economic stagnation and deflation, as well as excess demand and inflation.[8]

Decisions on general allocations of SDRs are made for successive basic periods of up to five years.

- The first basic period was for three years (1970–72), when a total of SDR 9.3 billion was allocated.
- There were no general allocations in the second basic period, 1973–77.

---

[7]See http://www.imf.org/external/np/tre/sdr/rates.

[8]The Articles of Agreement use only the term "allocation," and not "general allocation," which is used in this pamphlet to emphasize the difference with the one-time special allocation that will take place when the Fourth Amendment of the Articles becomes effective and with selective allocations that have been proposed.

BOX III.3. SDR INTEREST RATE: CALCULATION AND ACTUAL WEEKLY WEIGHTS

The interest rate on the SDR is defined as the sum of the multiplicative products in SDR terms of the currency amounts in the SDR valuation basket, the level of the interest rate on the financial instrument of each component currency in the basket, and the exchange rate of each currency against the SDR.

As in the valuation of the SDR, the currency amounts remain fixed for the five-year period following a revision in valuation basket. As a result, the actual weight of each financial instrument in the SDR interest rate changes on a weekly basis as a result of changes in both interest rates and exchange rates.

See example below. Note that these weights can differ from those in the valuation basket on the same date (see Box III.2) because the weights in the interest rate basket reflect changes in the levels of interest rates in each currency as well as change in exchange rates.

April 30, 2001

Currency	Currency Amount (1)	Interest Rate (2)	Exchange Rate Against the SDR[1] (3)	Product (1x2x3)	Actual Weight April 30, 2001
Euro	0.426	4.8363	0.70905500	1.4608	39
Japanese yen	21.0	0.0230	0.00636558	0.0031	0
Pounds sterling	0.0984	5.0952	1.13403000	0.5686	15
U. S. dollars	0.577	3.8500	0.78583100	1.7457	46
Total				3.78	100

[1]Exchange rates are expressed in terms of SDRs per currency units.

- In the third basic period, 1978–81, a total of SDR 12.1 billion was allocated.
- There have been no general allocations of SDRs since the third basic period.

The decision for a general allocation of SDRs follows a set procedure. First, if the Managing Director has determined that a proposal for SDR allocation has widespread support among SDR participants, he or she is required to make such a proposal at least six months before the commencement of a basic period, or within six months of a request for a proposal from the Executive Board or Board of Governors, or at such other times as specified in Article XVIII. Second, the Executive Board must agree with the proposal. Third, the Board of Governors has the power, by a majority of 85 percent of its total voting power, to approve or modify the proposal.[9]

Recent Proposals for SDR Allocations

A number of proposals have been advanced in recent years to enhance the role of the SDR in the international monetary system and to address specific issues. The principal proposals included a resumption of general allocations, a special allocation to correct inequities in the system by an amendment of the Articles, and a selective allocation that would redistribute a general allocation to help finance crisis lending.

In 1993, the Managing Director of the IMF proposed a general allocation of SDR 36 billion based on the finding of a long-term global need to supplement existing reserve assets. He also suggested that a means be found to redistribute voluntarily a portion of the new SDRs, subject to conditionality, to selected countries, including the countries that had joined the IMF since 1981 and, therefore, had never been allocated SDRs. The management and staff of the IMF maintained that the demand for reserves to hold had continued to grow but that the vast majority of the IMF's membership, accounting for almost half of IMF quotas, faced net costs of acquiring and holding reserves that were higher, in many cases significantly higher, than the true economic cost of creating reserves through SDR allocations. The existence of such a margin for a large proportion of the IMF membership was viewed as evidence of a global need to supplement existing reserve assets and that an SDR allocation was preferable to alternative sources of reserves.

However, the arguments put forth by the IMF staff for a general SDR allocation did not garner the necessary 85 percent voting majority of members required for passage. The reluctance of some large members to go along with the proposal reflected fundamental changes in the world economy that

---

[9]The procedures for cancellations of SDRs are broadly the same as those for allocations, except that cancellations are based on cumulative allocations rather than quotas. This ensures a uniform proportionate reduction for all members, regardless of the number of allocations in which they have participated.

they believed put into question the concept of a potential shortage of international reserves:

- The move to floating exchange rates.
- The growth of international capital markets and the expanded capacity of creditworthy national authorities to borrow.
- A concept of international liquidity that had become much broader than international reserves.

In 1993/94, the Executive Directors for the United Kingdom and the United States proposed, as an alternative to the Managing Director's proposal for a general allocation, an amendment of the Articles to provide a special allocation of SDRs. The purpose of the amendment was to address a perceived inequity that more than one-fifth of IMF members had never received an SDR allocation because they joined the IMF after the last allocation in 1981. The size and scope of the proposal was modified during the course of Executive Board discussions before a consensus was achieved in 1997.

In September 1997, the IMF's Board of Governors adopted a resolution to amend the Articles to allow for a special one-time allocation of SDRs. The proposed Fourth Amendment of the Articles would equalize all members' ratios of cumulative SDR allocations to quota (based on quotas following the Ninth Review of Quotas) at a common benchmark of 29.3 percent, which would result in a doubling of the outstanding stock of SDRs to SDR 42.8 billion. The amendment includes provisions to allow future new members to receive equal treatment and places the allocations of members with overdue obligations to the IMF in escrow accounts until their arrears to the IMF are cleared. The amendment would not affect the IMF's existing power to allocate SDRs on the basis of a finding of a long-term global need to supplement existing reserve assets. As of July 15, 2001, 108 IMF members with 72 percent of the total voting power had accepted the amendment (out of the 110 members with 85 percent of the voting power required for adoption).

A number of proposals for selective allocations have been advanced to use the SDR as a source of finance for conditional lending, particularly to enable the IMF to serve as a financial safety net or lender of last resort during financial crises. Under one form of these proposals, a general allocation of SDRs would occur under the existing authority of the Articles but the major industrial countries would agree voluntarily to onlend their allocated SDRs to the IMF or directly to countries undertaking IMF-supported programs. Interest in these proposals waned following agreement in 1998 on an

IMF quota increase as part of the Eleventh General Review of Quotas and the subsequent improvement in the IMF's liquidity position.

Participants and Prescribed Holders

SDRs are allocated only to IMF members that elect to be participants in the SDR Department and to observe the obligations of participants. Since April 7, 1980, all members of the IMF have been participants in the SDR Department. SDRs can be held by, but not allocated to, the GRA of the IMF and prescribed holders.

The IMF has the authority to prescribe, as other holders of SDRs, non-members, member countries that are not SDR Department participants, institutions that perform the functions of a central bank for more than one member, and other official entities. As of end-June 2001, there were 16 organizations approved as "prescribed holders."[10] These entities can acquire and use SDRs in transactions by agreement and in operations with participants and other holders. They cannot, however, receive allocations of SDRs or use SDRs in "transactions with designation." There is no general provision for prescribed holders to initiate transactions in SDRs with the GRA; however, in the case of those prescribed holders, if any, that are lenders to the IMF's GRA, it has been agreed that they may receive interest payments and repayments of principal from the IMF in SDRs.

Uses of SDRs

In the late 1970s and 1980s, the IMF took several measures to increase the liquidity and acceptability of the SDR. One step was to permit central banks to use SDRs freely on the basis of mutual agreement, without having to justify every transaction on the basis of balance of payments need. Another measure was to liberalize the requirement that countries that had used their SDRs

---

[10]The 16 prescribed holders are four central banks (the European Central Bank, the Bank of Central African States, the Central Bank of West African States, and the Eastern Caribbean Central Bank); three intergovernmental monetary institutions (the Bank for International Settlements, the Latin American Reserve Fund, and the Arab Monetary Fund); and nine development institutions (the African Development Bank, the African Development Fund, the Asian Development Bank, the East African Development Bank, the International Bank for Reconstruction and Development and the International Development Association (respectively, the "hard" and "soft" loan entities of the World Bank Group), the Islamic Development Bank, the Nordic Investment Bank, and the International Fund for Agricultural Development).

were expected eventually to partially "reconstitute" their holdings.[11] While the reconstitution requirement remained in place, the minimum required level of average holdings was reduced from 30 percent of cumulative allocations to 15 percent in 1979. In June 1981, the reconstitution requirement was suspended.

Originally, the IMF intended that SDRs be used only in spot transactions—that is, transactions with immediate settlement—between participants or participants and the IMF. But as part of the transition to a more market-oriented role for the SDR, the IMF broadened the scope of official transactions in SDRs to permit their use in swaps, forward transactions, loans, collateralization, and grants.[12] All of these steps were driven by the IMF's desire to promote the SDR as the "principal reserve asset" of the international monetary system, as required by the Second Amendment of the Articles. However, the IMF stopped short of issuing broad approval for the use of SDRs in any nonprescribed activity and thus retained a degree of control over the types of allowable transactions. In any case, the liberalized rules resulted in little new activity, as spot transactions have continued to account for almost all transactions in SDRs.

The SDR is used almost exclusively for transactions with the IMF and efforts to promote private uses have proven largely ineffective. A number of reasons have been advanced for this failure. As noted above, unlike currencies that represent a claim on their issuers, the SDR is not a claim on the IMF, but a claim on the freely usable currencies of IMF members. Moreover, the value of the SDR and its yield are not market determined, but reflect changes in the value or yield of its constituent currencies or financial instruments rather than a market clearing price. This means that the value and yield of the SDR are not free to respond to excess supply or demand pressures. As a result, the "market" for SDRs must be administratively managed by the IMF, as discussed in the next section. Finally, the private markets have developed alternative instruments that can provide the same kinds of currency hedge that could be achieved through use of the SDR.

---

[11]The reconstitution provision required that a country's holdings of SDRs must be at least a designated percentage of the cumulative allocation averaged over a five-year period.

[12]See *Users Guide to the SDR: A Manual of Transactions and Operations in SDRs* on the IMF website (http://www.imf.org/external/pubs/FT/usrgsdr/usercon.htm) for a detailed explanation of how SDRs can be used.

The IMF's own accounts are maintained in terms of SDRs and several other international organizations and conventions have also adopted the SDR as a unit of account.[13] As of April 30, 2001, the exchange rates of four IMF member countries were pegged to the SDR.

In summary, the SDR has not become more of a presence in the international monetary system for a number of reasons:

- First, the fixed exchange rate system for which the SDR was developed changed to a floating rate regime shortly after the introduction of the SDR. This, combined with the internationalization of capital markets, reduced the need for a central reserve asset like the SDR and helps explain why so few SDRs have been allocated.
- Second, the SDR is not a market-based asset. It has always been administratively controlled by the IMF in almost every respect, from its valuation and yield to who may hold it and what it may be used for. These restrictions, along with the development of new financial instruments in the markets themselves, help explain why the use of the SDR has not developed in private markets.

Operation of the SDR System

Flows of SDRs and the Central Role of the IMF

The IMF receives and disburses SDRs through the GRA, which is the focal point for the system-wide circulation of SDRs.

Inflows of SDRs into the GRA include:

- payments of charges (interest) owed to the GRA,[14]
- interest earned on GRA SDR holdings and assessments for the cost of conducting business with the SDR Department,
- repurchases, and
- the reserve asset portion (25 percent) of quota increases (Box III.4). [15]

---

[13]African Development Bank, Arab Monetary Fund, Asian Development Bank, Common Fund for Commodities, East African Development Bank, Economic Community of West African States, International Center for Settlement of Investment Disputes, International Fund for Agricultural Development, and Islamic Development Bank.

[14]The IMF's Articles require members to pay all charges due to the GRA in SDRs.

[15]The reserve asset portion of quota increases must be paid in SDRs, unless the IMF decides otherwise.

BOX III.4. BORROWING OF SDRs FOR PAYMENT OF THE RESERVE ASSET PORTION OF A QUOTA INCREASE

Members are required to pay 25 percent of quota increases in SDRs or currencies specified by the IMF, or in a combination of SDRs and currencies. The balances of the increases are payable in their own currencies.

In cases where the gross reserves and SDR holdings of members are low, the IMF, if requested, can make arrangements to assist members in making the payment of the reserve asset portion of their quota increases. This is done via a same-day loan, free of any interest, fee, or commission. Under the Eleventh General Review, five members with relatively large SDR holdings agreed to lend SDRs totaling SDR 2.8 billion to other members that had a need to borrow such SDRs. Similar arrangements existed under the Eighth and Ninth Quota Reviews, and can be arranged for ad hoc or selective quota increases outside of general reviews if needed.

The mechanism functions as follows:

(1) The member borrows SDRs from a member willing to lend SDRs.

(2) The member uses the borrowed SDRs to pay the reserve asset portion of its quota subscription.

(3) The member makes a reserve tranche purchase in the same amount (i.e., it pays in domestic currency equal to 25 percent of the increase in its own quota) and receives SDRs.

(4) The member uses the SDRs from (3) to repay the SDR loan to the lending member in (1) on the same day.

Outflows of SDRs from the GRA include:

- purchases,
- remuneration payments,
- loan repayments,
- interest payments on outstanding loans, and
- SDRs acquired by members to pay charges and assessments.

Members are not obliged to accept SDRs in any transaction except replenishment.[16] However, the IMF generally offers SDRs as an alternative

---

[16]The IMF may decide to use its SDR holdings to replenish its holdings of the currency of a participant in the SDR Department.

to currencies in all payments it makes to its members. Virtually all members holding IMF-remunerated reserve tranche positions choose to receive SDRs in quarterly remuneration payments,[17] and SDRs have been accepted in the repayment of loans and the payment of interest on outstanding loans. Members may acquire SDRs from the GRA for the payment of charges to the GRA and SDR Department and to pay assessments. The main flows of SDRs into and out of the GRA are presented in Figure III.2, which shows the relative proportions of these flows since 1990 and compares them to the level of transactions among participants and prescribed holders.

Members may accept SDRs in purchase transactions, and they may request to convert these to a usable currency in transactions with designation or transactions by agreement with other members, as discussed below.

The IMF recycles the stock of SDRs held in the GRA by:

- channeling SDRs directly from the GRA to debtor members who are making purchases from the IMF; and
- channeling SDRs indirectly from the holders of SDRs to other members who need to acquire SDRs to make payments to the IMF (i.e., charges and repurchases). The IMF may also assist members in buying or selling SDRs for reserve management purposes. Such transactions are usually carried out under the two-way arrangements to the extent that SDRs received in purchases from the GRA are converted into freely usable currencies.

The GRA is thus the primary force behind the circulation of SDRs — both to debtor members in connection with their purchases from the IMF and to creditor members in the payment of IMF borrowing and remuneration. The GRA's holdings of SDRs are subject to sharp spikes in the wake of reserve asset payments of quota increases (Figure III.3). The GRA's SDR holdings are returned to within a desired range mainly through transfers of SDRs for purchases and payments on IMF borrowing under its quarterly financial transactions plan. The Executive Board has periodically reviewed the level of the IMF's SDR holdings, particularly when circumstances warranted changes in the IMF's target range of SDR holdings. The last review was completed following the payment of quota increases under the Eleventh Review, when the Executive Board agreed that the IMF's SDR holdings should be maintained within a range of SDR 1.0–1.5 billion, which had proved adequate to meet the IMF's operational needs.

---

[17]Only one member has opted to receive remuneration payment in its own currency at present.

FIGURE III.2. SELECTED SDR TRANSACTIONS, FINANCIAL YEARS ENDED APRIL 30, 1990–2001

(In billions of SDRs)

Transactions Among Participants and Prescribed Holders

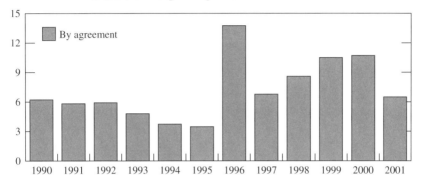

Transfers to IMF

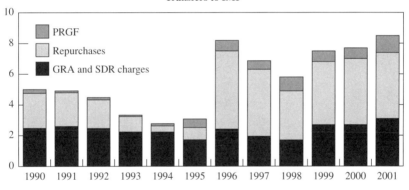

Transfers from IMF

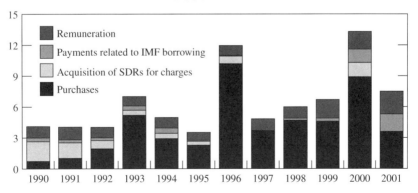

FIGURE III.3. IMF's HOLDINGS OF SDRs, JANUARY 1990–APRIL 2001

(In billions of SDRs; end of period)

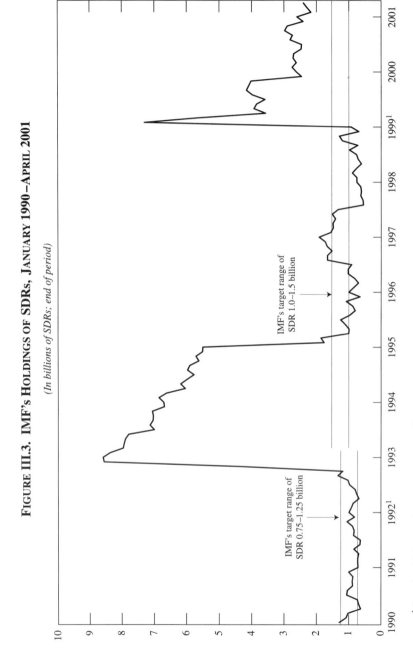

IMF's target range of
SDR 0.75–1.25 billion

IMF's target range of
SDR 1.0–1.5 billion

[1]Years in which quota increases went into effect.

System of Two-Way Arrangements

The two-way (buying and selling) arrangements are another important mechanism for circulating SDRs. The members with two-way or one-way arrangements effectively make a market in SDRs and increase the SDR's usability. The two-way arrangements enable members to acquire SDRs in exchange for freely usable currencies (mainly U.S. dollars and euros in practice), without having to claim a balance of payments need. Since the main attraction of the SDR as a reserve asset is the claim it represents on freely usable currencies, the system of two-way arrangements enhances the attractiveness of the SDR.

Each two-way arrangement specifies a range of SDR holdings within which transactions may be initiated, the specific currencies to be exchanged, the date of settlement (normally two or three business days), the minimum and maximum amounts of individual transactions, and the notice period required before initiating a particular transaction. The first two-way arrangement was created in February 1986, and, by the end of 1987, nine two-way arrangements were in place. At present, there are 13 market-makers with two-way arrangements and one sell-only arrangement. The combined holdings ranges of these arrangements total about SDR 3½ billion. The sell-only arrangement stipulates a floor and any holdings in excess of that minimum are available for sale.

The supply of SDRs for the two-way arrangements comes mainly from the resale of SDRs from members receiving SDRs in purchases from the IMF. The demand for SDRs comes from members that need them for the settlement of their financial obligations to the IMF. The scope of recirculation of SDRs under the two-way arrangements is limited by three factors:
- the size of SDR transfers under new IMF credits;
- the extent to which members receiving such credits convert SDRs into currency; and
- the absorptive capacity (i.e., the difference between members' current holdings and the maximum limits) available under the two-way arrangements.[18]

---

[18]For example, in a period of little or no new extensions of IMF credit, such as in the late 1980s, members requiring SDRs to settle their IMF obligations had to turn to the IMF itself or resort to ad hoc approaches to other members.

111

In general, the scope for recirculation of SDRs is much greater when they are held by members with two-way arrangements (Box III.5).

The role of the IMF in transactions by agreement is to act as an intermediary matching participants in this managed market. The two-way arrangements allow the IMF to initiate purchases and sales of SDRs on behalf of any participant in the SDR Department against usable currencies, subject to the constraint that all transactions take place at the official SDR exchange rate for the currency involved. As the market does not always clear, the supply and demand for SDRs must be managed through the judicious design of the quarterly financial transaction plans. The limited supply of SDRs is assigned primarily to meet the demand for members' obligations that must be paid in SDRs. Ad hoc requests from members to acquire SDRs for reserve management purposes are frequently difficult to meet.

Pattern of SDR Holdings

The use of SDRs in certain transactions (e.g., payment of charges, repurchases, related payments on IMF borrowings, and remuneration) has resulted in increasing imbalances in the distribution of SDRs among members. The distribution of SDR holdings is skewed toward a few creditor members, mainly the industrial countries. One member holds over one-third of the current outstanding stock of SDRs. Another relatively large group of members — predominantly debtor countries who have experienced balance of payments difficulties over a long period of time — typically holds relatively small amounts of SDRs in terms of its cumulative allocations. A third group of members has shifted between creditor to debtor positions, and maintained its holdings of SDRs at an average level of about 60 percent of its cumulative allocations in recent years (Table III.2).

Financial Statements of the SDR Department

The strict separation of the IMF's General and SDR Departments implies that their financial accounts be kept separately. The basic structure of the SDR Department's balance sheet (Table III.3) is quite simple. Since interest payments and receipts cancel out for the department as a whole, it is convenient to keep the accounts on a net basis.

Box III.5. The Circulation of SDRs

• All IMF members and participants in the SDR Department receive SDRs at the time of SDR allocations.

• The GRA receives SDRs from members meeting obligations (A) and making reserve asset payments associated with periodic quota increases (B).

• The GRA transfers SDRs mainly to members under IMF arrangements (C) and makes remuneration payments to creditor members (D).

• Most transactions intermediated through two-way arrangements stem from the resale of SDRs received under IMF arrangements (E) or through the purchases of SDRs to meet obligations to the IMF (F).

• Receipt and payment of net SDR interest occurs among members (G), although the IMF and prescribed holders also receive interest on their SDR holdings.

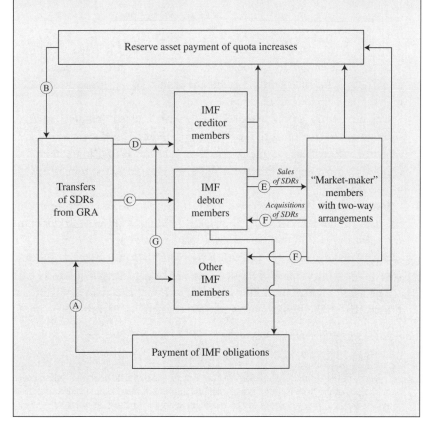

TABLE III.2. SDR HOLDINGS OF SELECTED GROUPS
OF COUNTRIES[1]

(In percent of cumulative allocations)

	1983	1987	October 1992[2]	1997	1998[2]	June 1999[3]	1999	2000	April 2001
IMF creditors (26)	86	120	123	113	115	107	104	101	105
IMF debtors (103)	10	22	18	48	41	34	39	40	29
Other members (54)	58	73	59	81	75	60	68	80	82

[1]Number of members is shown in parentheses.
[2]Before quota increase (Ninth and Eleventh Reviews).
[3]After quota increase (Eleventh Review).

The asset side of the balance sheet shows the position of debtors to the SDR Department—that is, members who have exchanged some of their SDRs for freely usable currency and whose holdings of SDRs therefore fall short of their cumulative allocations. The accrued interest receivable from these debtor members on the asset side is the mirror image of the accrued interest payable to creditors on the liability side.

The final entry on the asset side represents interest and assessments due from members in arrears to the SDR Department. If sufficient SDRs are not received when these payments are due, additional SDRs are temporarily created to pay them. When the arrears are cleared, these temporary SDRs are canceled.

Participants with holdings above allocations assume a creditor position in the department and therefore their SDR holdings in excess of their cumulative allocations are liabilities of the department, as are any holdings of prescribed holders and the IMF (GRA), which do not receive allocations. Interest payable to these creditors is accrued and paid on a quarterly basis.[19]

The income statement of the SDR Department is equally straightforward (Table III.4). The department's income consists of interest payments from

---

[19]As the balance sheet is shown on the last day of the financial year, the interest accrued over the previous three months is shown. This amount would be paid out to creditors on May 1, with the figure reverting to zero to begin accruals for the next quarter.

TABLE III.3. BALANCE SHEET OF THE SDR DEPARTMENT,
AS OF APRIL 30, 2001

(In millions of SDRs)

Assets		Liabilities	
Participants with holdings below allocations:		Participants with holdings above allocations:	
Allocations	12,646	SDR holdings	14,690
less: SDR holdings	3,866	less: allocations	8,787
Allocations in excess of holdings	8,780	Holdings in excess of allocations	5,903
		Holdings by GRA	2,437
		Holdings by prescribed holders	538
Interest receivable	215	Interest payable	216
Overdue assessments and interest	98		
Total assets	9,094	Total liabilities	9,094

Note: Numbers may not add to totals due to rounding.

debtors and assessments paid by members for the administrative expenses incurred in operating the department. The department's expenses consist of interest payments to the creditors in the system and the reimbursement to the IMF for the administration of the department. As revenue and expenditure are always equal, net income is always zero.

Seminar on the Future of the SDR

In 1995, the IMF Interim Committee (now the IMFC) "requested the IMF to initiate a broad review, with the involvement of outside experts, of the role and functions of the SDR in light of changes in the international financial system." The IMF convened a seminar in March 1996 involving the participation of policymakers, academic economists, and other influential leaders,

TABLE III.4. INCOME STATEMENT OF THE SDR DEPARTMENT,
FINANCIAL YEAR ENDED APRIL 30, 2001

(In millions of SDRs)

Income	
Net interest from participants with holdings below allocations	400
Assessment on SDR allocations	2
	403
Expenses	
Interest on SDR holdings	
Net interest to participants with holdings above allocations	261
GRA	113
Prescribed holders	27
Administrative expenses	2
	403
Net income	0

Note: Numbers may not add to totals due to rounding.

along with the IMF staff, to examine the role of the SDR, the rationale for allocating SDRs, the criteria for distributing SDRs, and the characteristics of the SDR.[20] The seminar helped to inform the subsequent Executive Board discussions on the principal allocation proposals even though the seminar participants were divided on many key issues and expressed doubt about whether it was realistic to expect the SDR to become the principal reserve asset in the international monetary system. There was, however, general support to maintain the present role of the SDR.

---

[20]The *Future of the SDR in Light of Changes in the International Financial System*, ibid. (see footnote 2).

IV

Financial Assistance for
Low-Income Members

The IMF provides financial assistance to low-income member countries in two ways: through concessional lending under the Poverty Reduction and Growth Facility (PRGF) and through debt relief under the Heavily Indebted Poor Countries (HIPC) Initiative. The PRGF (which replaced the ESAF in 1999) supports economic programs, which strengthen substantially and in a sustainable manner balance of payments positions and foster durable growth, leading to higher living standards and a reduction in poverty. The HIPC Initiative helps countries achieve a sustainable external debt position. Resources for financing these initiatives, which are separate from the IMF's general resources generated from quota subscriptions, have been provided through contributions by a broad segment of the IMF's membership, as well as by the IMF itself. These resources are administered under the PRGF and PRGF-HIPC Trusts, for which the IMF acts as Trustee. This chapter describes the financing arrangements for the PRGF and for the HIPC Initiative.

An important part of IMF assistance to low-income members is technical and capacity-building support made available at the request of such countries and at no cost to them. The IMF's technical assistance program is discussed briefly in Chapter V.[1]

Overview of Concessional Assistance

The IMF's concessional financial assistance to low-income members has been strengthened progressively over the past 25 years. The initial assistance, financed entirely through the profits from the IMF's gold sales in 1976–80, was disbursed with low conditionality, first through Trust Fund loans and later through Structural Adjustment Facility (SAF) loans. Since 1987, concessional loans financed in large part by bilateral contributions have been extended through facilities with the equivalence of upper credit tranche conditionality through the ESAF and, since 1999, the PRGF.

---

[1]See the section on "Voluntary Safeguards" in Chapter V. For more information, see the "Policy Statement on IMF Technical Assistance," March 31, 2000, which is posted on the IMF website (http://www.imf.org/external/np/ta/2000/index.htm).

- In 1976, the IMF initiated concessional operations through the establishment of the Trust Fund, which drew upon the profits generated from the sale of part of the IMF's gold holdings in 1976–80 and provided concessional loans to low-income developing countries for balance of payments support.[2]
- In 1986, the IMF established the SAF to provide concessional assistance to low-income countries by recycling resources lent under the Trust Fund.[3]
- In 1987, the IMF established the ESAF to foster stronger adjustment and reform measures than those under the SAF and to augment the resources available for this purpose. In contrast to the Trust Fund and SAF, the loan and subsidy resources were provided primarily by bilateral contributors.
- In 1996, the IMF and World Bank jointly launched the HIPC Initiative to reduce the external debt burden of eligible poor and heavily indebted countries to a sustainable level.
- In September 1999, the HIPC Initiative was enhanced to provide faster, deeper, and broader debt relief and the links between debt relief and poverty reduction were strengthened.[4] In October 1999, the Executive Board decided to change the names of the ESAF and ESAF Trust to the Poverty Reduction and Growth Facility (PRGF) and the Poverty Reduction and Growth Facility Trust (PRGF Trust), respectively, and to broaden the objectives of the renamed facility. The decision became effective on November 22, 1999, when all contributors to the Trust had consented to the change.[5]
- In September 1999, agreement was also reached on a financing package for the HIPC Initiative and for a continuation of the PRGF for a four-year period (the so-called interim PRGF) expected to begin in 2002

---

[2]Of the $4.6 billion in profits from the gold sales, $1.3 billion was distributed to developing country members of the IMF in proportion to their quotas, while $3.3 billion was made available for concessional lending through the Trust Fund.

[3]See Joslin Landell-Mills, *Helping the Poor: The IMF's New Facilities for Structural Adjustment* (Washington: International Monetary Fund, rev. ed., 1992).

[4]For a more thorough discussion of the Enhanced HIPC Initiative, see David Andrews, Anthony Boote, Syed S. Rizavi, and Sukhwinder Singh, *Debt Relief for Low-Income Countries: The Enhanced HIPC Initiative*, IMF Pamphlet Series No. 51 (Washington: International Monetary Fund, 2000).

[5]See "IMF Lending to Poor Countries—How Does the PRGF Differ from the ESAF?" (International Monetary Fund, Issues Brief, 01/06, April 2001).

after the full commitment of existing PRGF resources and before the onset of self-sustained PRGF operations.

- Loan resources of SDR 4–4.5 billion for interim PRGF lending are now being mobilized.

- In May 2001, the IMF established an account to gather resources for providing an interest subsidy on post-conflict emergency assistance to PRGF-eligible countries. The grants from this subsidy account will reduce the annual rate of charge for purchases from the GRA under the post-conflict emergency assistance facility to 0.5 percent (same rate of charge as the interest on use of PRGF resources).

- After 2005, it is anticipated that a substantial proportion of concessional lending will be provided through self-sustained PRGF operations financed by the IMF's own resources accumulating in the Reserve Account of the PRGF Trust. These resources, which derive from the IMF's gold sales in the late 1970s and related investment income, will become available as PRGF lenders are repaid and the security provided by the Reserve Account is no longer needed.

An overview of the financing of the IMF's concessional assistance is summarized in Box IV.1, while Figure IV.1 shows the level and composition of IMF concessional lending from its inception to the present.

PRGF and HIPC Operations

The IMF acts as Trustee for the PRGF and PRGF-HIPC Trusts, and through these Trusts administers the various resources supporting PRGF and HIPC operations. In this capacity, the IMF mobilizes and manages resources for both Trusts.

PRGF Trust

Eligibility, Terms, and Access for PRGF Resources

In practice, the IMF has relied on the level of per capita income and eligibility under the International Development Association (IDA), the concessional lending arm of the World Bank, to determine eligibility for PRGF loans. However, there is no automatic link between PRGF and IDA eligibility and it is up to the Executive Board of the IMF to establish the list of PRGF-eligible

---

Box IV.1. Overview of Financing for the IMF's Concessional Assistance

PRGF Trust

• Established as the ESAF Trust in 1987 and enlarged in 1994, with loan resources of SDR 11.4 billion provided by 17 bilateral lenders and subsidy contributions by a larger number of IMF member countries.

• Loans to the Trust are secured by a Reserve Account, which is financed through a recycling of profits from gold sales in the late 1970s (i.e., reflows of SAF and Trust Fund repayments) and investment returns on balances held in the Account; the rights accumulation gold pledge (see Chapter II); and an informal statement on security to lenders by the Managing Director (see text on the Reserve Account).

PRGF-HIPC Trust

• The framework for the HIPC Initiative and the interim PRGF was agreed in 1996. Agreement was reached in late 1999 on the financing of the subsidy required for the interim PRGF (during 2002–05) and the IMF's participation in the HIPC Initiative. Contributions are provided by 94 member countries and the IMF.

• The framework and sources of loan resources for the interim PRGF of SDR 4–4.5 billion were not identified when the PRGF-HIPC Trust was established. Progress has been made in mobilizing such resources through new bilateral lending, but further efforts are needed to secure the full amount required.

Self-Sustained PRGF

• Expected to begin operations in 2006 financed through a revolving use of the resources accumulating in the Reserve Account of the PRGF Trust. No interest subsidy contributions or loan resources will be needed from bilateral contributions.

	Loans (In billions of SDRs)	Commitment Periods	Status of Financing (In billions of SDRs) Principal	Subsidies
PRGF Trust	11.4	1988–2001	Financed	Financed
PRGF-HIPC Trust Interim PRGF	4–4.5	2002–05	3.3[1] (committed)	Fully committed; mostly effective
HIPC Initiative	(for delivery of grants or loans)			Fully committed; mostly effective
Self-sustained PRGF	0.7/year in perpetuity	From 2006 onward	Financed	Self-financed

[1]As of end-June 2001.

FIGURE IV.1. OUTSTANDING IMF CONCESSIONAL CREDIT BY FACILITY,
FINANCIAL YEARS ENDED APRIL 30, 1976–2001

(*In millions of SDRs*)

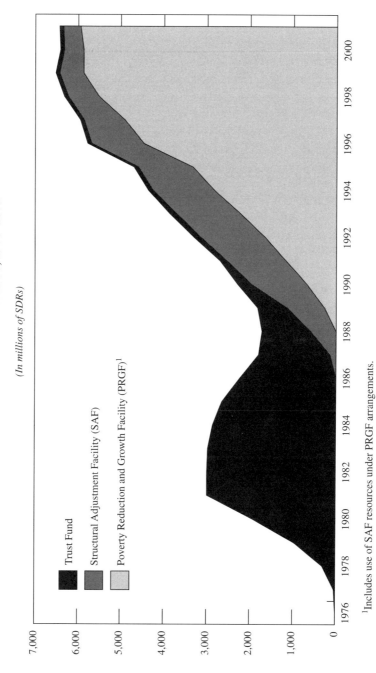

Trust Fund

Structural Adjustment Facility (SAF)

Poverty Reduction and Growth Facility (PRGF)[1]

[1]Includes use of SAF resources under PRGF arrangements.

countries.[6] Since 1987, many countries, including some countries in transition, have become members, while others have been removed from the list. Currently, 77 members of the IMF are eligible for the PRGF (Box IV.2).

PRGF loans are provided under three-year PRGF arrangements (with a possibility of a one-year extension), with annual programs for each of the three years. Disbursements under PRGF arrangements are tied to performance criteria and reviews normally set for semiannual periods, although reviews can also be quarterly when more frequent monitoring is appropriate. Loans under the PRGF carry an annual interest rate of 0.5 percent, with equal repayments made semiannually, beginning 5½ years and ending 10 years after disbursement.

PRGF-supported programs are framed around a comprehensive, nationally owned Poverty Reduction Strategy Paper (PRSP) prepared by the borrowing country government and based on a process involving the active participation of civil society, nongovernmental organizations, donors, and international institutions. These PRSPs are then endorsed in their respective areas of responsibility by the Executive Boards of the IMF and the World Bank as the basis for the institutions' concessional loans and for relief under the enhanced HIPC Initiative. PRGF-supported programs emerge directly from the PRSPs and macroeconomic policies in such programs are integrated with social and sectoral objectives, to ensure that plans are mutually supportive and consistent with a common set of objectives to spur growth and reduce poverty. PRGF-supported programs embody budgets that are pro-poor with a reorientation of government spending toward the social sectors, basic infrastructure, or other activities that demonstrably benefit the poor. PRGF-supported programs also emphasize improvements in governance as a fundamental underpinning for macroeconomic stability, sustainable growth, and poverty reduction. The primary focus is on better management of public resources, achieving greater transparency, active public scrutiny, and generally increased government accountability in fiscal management.

An eligible country may borrow up to 140 percent of its IMF quota under a three-year arrangement, although this limit may be increased under exceptional circumstances to a maximum of 185 percent of quota. Access under individual PRGF arrangements is determined on the basis of the balance of

---

[6] The current cutoff point for IDA eligibility is a 1999 per capita GNP level of $885.

Box IV.2. PRGF- and HIPC-Eligible Countries

1. Afghanistan, I.S. of
2. Albania
3. Angola*
4. Armenia
5. Azerbaijan
6. Bangladesh
7. Benin*
8. Bhutan
9. Bolivia*
10. Bosnia and
    Herzegovina
11. Burkina Faso*
12. Burundi*
13. Cambodia
14. Cameroon*
15. Cape Verde
16. Central African
    Republic*
17. Chad*
18. Comoros
19. Congo, Democratic
    Republic of the*
20. Congo,
    Republic of*
21. Côte d'Ivoire*
22. Djibouti
23. Dominica
24. Eritrea

25. Ethiopia*
26. Gambia, The*
27. Georgia
28. Ghana*
29. Grenada
30. Guinea*
31. Guinea-Bissau*
32. Guyana*
33. Haiti
34. Honduras*
35. India
36. Kenya*[1]
37. Kiribati
38. Kyrgyz Republic
39. Lao, P.D.R.*[2]
40. Lesotho
41. Liberia*
42. Macedonia, F.Y.R.
43. Madagascar*
44. Malawi*
45. Maldives
46. Mali*
47. Mauritania*
48. Moldova
49. Mongolia
50. Mozambique*
51. Myanmar*
52. Nepal

53. Nicaragua*
54. Niger*
55. Nigeria
56. Pakistan
57. Rwanda*
58. Samoa
59. São Tomé and
    Príncipe*
60. Senegal*
61. Sierra Leone*
62. Solomon Islands
63. Somalia*
64. Sri Lanka
65. St. Lucia
66. St. Vincent and
    the Grenadines
67. Sudan*
68. Tajikistan
69. Tanzania*
70. Togo*
71. Tonga
72. Uganda*
73. Vanuatu
74. Vietnam*
75. Yemen,
    Republic of*[1]
76. Zambia*
77. Zimbabwe

---

* HIPC-eligible countries.

[1]One of two HIPC-eligible countries that have sustainable debt as defined in the Initiative. In July 2000, the IMF and World Bank confirmed that the Republic of Yemen does not need HIPC Initiative assistance to reach debt sustainability.

[2]Country has indicated that it does not want to make use of the HIPC Initiative.

payments need of the member, the strength of the adjustment program, the member's outstanding use of IMF credit, and the record of such use in the past. Access is subject to review, both at the approval of a three-year arrangement and at the periodic reviews thereafter. Over the years the access policy has evolved to provide for different access levels according to circumstances. There is substantial differentiation in access in individual cases because of a variety of factors:

- In some cases, where there is a balance of payments need, a convincing strengthening of the adjustment effort, and capacity to repay, actual access within existing limits tends to be higher now than in the past, with the expectation that continued strong performance should both elicit support from others and permit a steady decline over time in the need for exceptional balance of payments support, including from the PRGF. Where the balance of payments need is not clear cut, lower access is set appropriately on a case-by-case basis.

- No access is appropriate in cases that have relatively weak track records and are not able to implement sufficiently strong policies. In these circumstances, the IMF seeks to continue to play an active role through the provision of policy advice and technical assistance in helping countries elaborate and implement strong policy reforms that could eventually merit support from the IMF and other sources.

- Since repeat users are likely to have IMF credit outstanding, access is expected to be lower than for first-time users in otherwise similar situations; this does not, however, preclude an IMF response through higher access in support of suitably strong policies.

- For poor countries that are heavily indebted, greater emphasis is given to the outstanding use of IMF credit in setting access. There are wide variations across countries in the ratio of quotas to exports, which implies that similar access levels in relation to quotas result in widely differing debt-service burdens to the IMF. Thus, access in individual cases is more closely tied to countries' current and prospective payments capacity than to quotas.

- The "blending" of concessional PRGF with market-based GRA resources through parallel arrangements continues to be an option for those countries that have the capacity to service nonconcessional debt, allowing greater scope for access by others more in need of PRGF resources.

Sources and Uses of Financing

PRGF operations are conducted through three accounts within the PRGF Trust: the Loan Account, Reserve Account, and Subsidy Account (Figure IV.2.)

The Loan Account borrows resources generally at market-related interest rates from central banks, governments, and official institutions, and lends them on a pass-through basis to PRGF-eligible countries.[7] At the end of April 2001, the IMF had entered into 28 bilateral borrowing agreements with 17 creditors for SDR 11.4 billion for on-lending to PRGF-eligible members; Saudi Arabia has provided additional loan resources through an associated lending agreement between the Saudi Fund for Development and the IMF (Table IV.1). Most of these loans are remunerated at a six-month SDR interest rate, with a maturity typically set to match the maturity profile of loan repayments from borrowing members (i.e., with a 5½-year grace period and 10-year maturity).

Since July 1988, 54 of the 77 PRGF-eligible members have made use of PRGF loans. Many of these members have had multiple PRGF or ESAF arrangements as they endeavor to achieve sustainable economic growth and poverty reduction. At end-April 2001, about SDR 10 billion of the total available loan resources of SDR 11.4 billion was committed to borrowing members, and SDR 7.9 billion was disbursed. It is expected that the remainder of resources will be fully committed around late 2001 or early 2002.

The Reserve Account of the PRGF Trust is designed to:

- provide security to the lenders to the Loan Account of the Trust in the event of delayed or nonpayment by PRGF borrowers;[8]
- meet temporary mismatches between repayments from borrowers and payments to lenders; and
- cover the IMF's costs of administering PRGF operations.[9]

---

[7]Lenders have extended resources to the PRGF Trust on various interest terms, in some cases at highly concessional rates.

[8]Additional security to lenders includes the gold pledge for rights accumulation programs financed from the PRGF Trust (see Chapter II) and an informal statement of the Managing Director of the IMF in 1987 which made clear that the IMF would take "all such initiatives as might be necessary" to ensure repayment of PRGF loans to PRGF lenders. This statement is understood to include the possible use of a portion of the IMF's holdings of gold.

[9]In April 1998 and April 1999, the IMF's Executive Board decided that no reimbursement would be made from the Reserve Account to the GRA for the annual cost of administering the PRGF Trust for FY1998–2000 and that, instead, an equivalent amount would be transferred from the Reserve Account to the PRGF-HIPC Trust. On December 8, 1999, the Executive Board agreed to extend the earlier decision to cover FY2001–04. These transfers are estimated to amount to SDR 0.6 billion for FY1998–2004.

FIGURE IV.2. FINANCIAL STRUCTURE OF THE PRGF TRUST

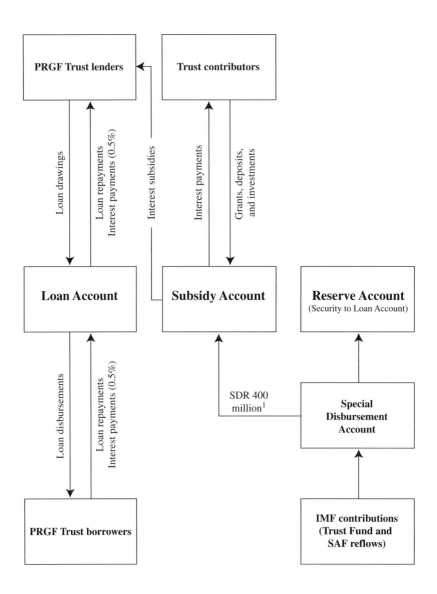

[1] A one-time transfer.

TABLE IV.1. LENDERS TO THE PRGF TRUST, AS OF APRIL 30, 2001[1]

(In millions of SDRs)

1. National Bank of Belgium	200
2. Government of Canada	700
3. Government of China	100
4. National Bank of Denmark	100
5. Central Bank of Egypt	100
6. Agence Française de Développement	1,900
7. Kreditanstalt für Wiederaufbau (Germany)	1,750
8. Bank of Italy	830
9. Japan Bank for International Cooperation	4,350
10. Bank of Korea	93
11. The Netherlands Bank	250
12. Bank of Norway	150
13. OPEC Fund for International Development[2]	40
14. Bank of Spain	341
15. Government of Spain	67
16. Swiss Confederation	200
17. Swiss National Bank	152
Total	11,322

Note: Numbers may not add to total due to rounding.

[1]Excluding associated loans from the Saudi Fund for Development in the amount of SDR 49.5 million.

[2]The loan commitment is for the SDR equivalent of $50 million valued at the exchange rate of April 30, 2001.

As of end-April 2001, the balance in the Reserve Account amounted to SDR 2.7 billion, equivalent to 47 percent of outstanding obligations to PRGF lenders. Thus far, the PRGF Trust has experienced a good track record of payments by PRGF borrowers, with only two cases of principal arrears exceeding one month in duration.

The balance in the Reserve Account is projected to be sufficient to cover all outstanding PRGF Trust obligations to lenders by around 2007. Factors that affect the pace of further accumulation of balances in the Reserve Account include:

- repayments of SAF and Trust Fund loans, including those by countries with protracted arrears to the IMF;
- the investment return on resources in the account; and
- the level of transfers to meet the cost of administering PRGF operations.

The primary factor driving Reserve Account accumulations is the investment return on resources in the account. The annual rate of return on investments in the account has averaged about 4.8 percent over the life of the PRGF Trust through end-April 2001. Assuming that the return on investment remains at about 5 percent a year, the cumulative balance in the Reserve Account is projected to increase from SDR 2.7 billion at end-April 2001 to SDR 3.9 billion at end-2005, when the self-sustained PRGF is expected to begin (Figure IV.3)

The Subsidy Account of the PRGF Trust receives contributions from bilateral sources and contributions from the IMF's own resources to subsidize the rate of interest on PRGF loans to borrowers at ½ of 1 percent a year. These resources finance the difference between the market rate of interest paid to PRGF Trust lenders and the rate of interest of ½ of 1 percent a year paid by the borrowing members. Subsidy resources are typically provided through either grant contributions or deposits and investments placed by contributors with the PRGF Trust at below-market interest rates. In the latter case, the interest rate differential between the rate of interest earned on the deposit or investment by the PRGF Trust and the rate of interest paid to the contributor represents a subsidy contribution to the PRGF Trust.[10] As of end-April 2001, the Subsidy Account had received contributions, including investment income, totaling SDR 3.0 billion, of which SDR 2.6 billion was provided by 40 bilateral contributors, with the rest (SDR 0.4 billion) provided by the IMF.

The adequacy of the resources in the Subsidy Account to support PRGF lending depends critically on the future rate of interest paid to PRGF Trust lenders, the investment return on balances held in the Subsidy Account, and the level and pace of PRGF lending. Based on an assumed annual investment return of 5 percent and a similar interest rate on loans extended by PRGF Trust lenders over the remaining life of the Trust (around 2015), subsidy resources are expected to exceed estimated needs by a small margin.

---

[10]In certain cases, the PRGF Trust may receive subsidy contributions through the provision by lenders of loan resources to the Trust at below-market interest rates. The IMF has also, at contributors' requests, agreed to receive and place deposits or investments in the Administered Contribution Account.

FIGURE IV.3. PRGF TRUST: PROJECTED OUTSTANDING OBLIGATIONS AND RESERVE ACCOUNT BALANCES

(In billions of SDRs)

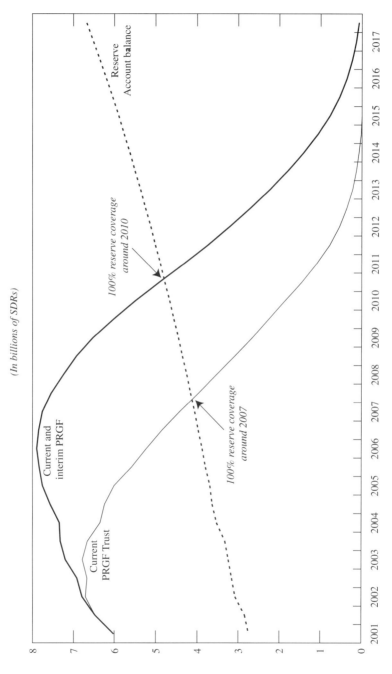

Financial Statements of the PRGF Trust

The sources and uses of resources of the PRGF Trust are summarized in its balance sheet (Table IV.2). The sources are identified as "Resources and liabilities," while the uses are shown as "Assets." The bulk of resources reflects borrowings and the accumulated resources of the Reserve Account. The major assets are loans receivable, reflecting outstanding PRGF loans to low-income countries, and investments of the Reserve Account.

The Income Statement for the PRGF Trust for FY2001 is shown in Table IV.3.

PRGF-HIPC Trust

Resources for debt relief under the HIPC Initiative and subsidized PRGF loans are administered by the IMF under the PRGF-HIPC Trust, established in February 1997.

The HIPC Initiative

The IMF and the World Bank jointly launched the Heavily Indebted Poor Countries (HIPC) Initiative to support a growing recognition by the international community that the external debt burden of a number of low-income countries, mostly in Africa, had become unsustainable. The HIPC Initiative entails coordinated action by the international financial community, including multilateral institutions, to reduce the external debt burden of these countries to sustainable levels. The Initiative complements traditional debt relief mechanisms, concessional financing, and the pursuit of sound economic policies, which together are designed to place these countries on a sustainable external footing.

Under the HIPC framework, the IMF and the World Bank determine the eligibility of a member and the amount of HIPC assistance to be committed at the decision point—the point at which the member completes its first record of good policy performance under programs supported by the IMF and the World Bank (Box IV.3).[11] Beginning from the decision point, an eligible member may receive interim assistance from the IMF of up to

---

[11]The IMF's Executive Board has agreed to be flexible in assessing the track record prior to the decision point in order to deliver interim HIPC assistance to eligible post-conflict countries as rapidly as possible.

TABLE IV.2. PRGF TRUST: COMBINED BALANCE SHEETS,
AS OF APRIL 30, 2001
(In millions of SDRs)

	Loan Account	Reserve Account	Subsidy Account	Combined
Assets				
Cash and cash equivalents	159.6	519.7	181.1	860.4
Investments	215.5	2,200.5	1,762.2	4,178.3
Loans receivable	5,899.5	—	—	5,899.5
Accrued account transfers	27.2	30.6	(57.9)	—
Interest receivable	13.2	5.1	0.4	18.7
Total assets	6,315.1	2,756.0	1,885.8	10,956.8
Resources and liabilities				
Borrowing	6,244.0	—	108.8	6,352.8
Interest payable	71.0	—	1.7	72.7
Other liabilities	—	12.5	—	12.5
Total liabilities	6,315.1	12.5	110.5	6,438.0
Resources	—	2,743.5	1,775.3	4,518.8
Total resources and liabilities	6,315.1	2,756.0	1,885.8	10,956.8

Note: Numbers may not add to totals due to rounding.

20 percent annually and 60 percent in total (25 percent and 75 percent, respectively, in exceptional circumstances) of the committed amount of HIPC assistance between the decision point and the floating completion point — the point when the member has fulfilled all policy-related conditions for HIPC assistance. Remaining undistributed HIPC Initiative assistance is delivered at the completion point.

The IMF provides its share of assistance under the HIPC Initiative to eligible members in the form of grants or loans or both, which are used to help meet debt-service payments to the IMF. So far, HIPC Initiative assistance has been extended only through grants. Between the decision point and the floating completion point, interim assistance may be provided in annual installments to an account of the member administered by the IMF. These resources are used for debt-service payments to the IMF as they fall due. The member's account earns interest on any balance during the interim period. At the completion point, the IMF deposits the remaining amount of

TABLE IV.3. PRGF TRUST: COMBINED INCOME STATEMENTS,
FINANCIAL YEAR ENDED APRIL 30, 2001

(In millions of SDRs)

	Loan Account	Reserve Account	Subsidy Account	Combined
Balance, April 30, 2000	—	2,558.4	1,747.4	4,305.7
Investment income	—	155.8	116.6	272.5
Interest on loans	28.9	—	—	28.9
Interest expense	(237.5)	—	(2.1)	(239.6)
Other expenses	(0.1)	(1.6)	—	(1.6)
Operational income (loss)	(208.7)	154.3	114.5	60.1
Contributions	—	—	127.0	127.0
Net income	(208.7)	154.3	241.5	187.1
Transfers from SDA	—	25.9	—	25.9
Transfers between				
Reserve and Subsidy Accounts	—	1.1	(1.1)	—
Loan and Reserve Accounts	(3.9)	3.9	—	—
Loan and Subsidy Accounts	212.6	—	(212.6)	—
Net changes in resources	—	185.1	27.9	213.0
Balance, April 30, 2001	—	2,743.5	1,775.3	4,518.8

Note: Numbers may not add to totals due to rounding.

undisbursed committed assistance to the member's account. After the completion point is reached, the member will continue to draw on the resources of its account for debt-service payments to the IMF according to a schedule agreed between the IMF and the member.

Continuation of PRGF Lending

The framework for the PRGF envisages continued commitments to borrowers under the current PRGF Trust through late 2001 or early 2002, to be followed by a four-year interim PRGF with a commitment capacity of about SDR 1 billion a year. The objective of the interim PRGF will be the same as that of the current PRGF, that is, to promote sustainable economic growth and achieve durable poverty reduction. The subsidy needs of the

---

BOX IV.3. ENHANCED HIPC INITIATIVE: QUALIFICATION CRITERIA

A country must satisfy a set of criteria to qualify for special assistance. Specifically, it must:
- be eligible for concessional assistance from the IMF and World Bank;
- face an unsustainable debt burden, notwithstanding available debt-relief mechanisms such as Naples terms (where low-income countries can receive a reduction of eligible external debt of 67 percent in net present value (NPV) terms), defined as:
  - a debt-to-export ratio of more than 150 percent (in NPV terms), or
  - a debt-to-government revenue ratio of more than 250 percent (in NPV terms)
- establish a track record of reform and sound policies through programs supported by the IMF and the World Bank.

All countries requesting HIPC Initiative assistance are normally expected to (1) have a Poverty Reduction Strategy Paper (PRSP) developed through a broad-based participatory process and accepted by the Executive Boards of the IMF and World Bank by the time of the decision point, and (2) have made progress in implementing this strategy for at least one year by the time of the completion point.

---

interim PRGF are included in the financing arrangements for the PRGF-HIPC Trust, while new loan resources are being sought from bilateral lenders.

Sources and Uses of Financing

The financing required for the IMF's cost of HIPC assistance and interim PRGF subsidies are estimated at SDR 3.0 billion in end-2000 net present value (NPV) terms,[12] with the HIPC Initiative accounting for about two-thirds of the total. These financing requirements are to be met through bilateral contributions to the IMF amounting to SDR 1.2 billion in NPV terms and contributions by the IMF itself of SDR 1.8 billion in NPV terms (Table IV.4).

---

[12]These estimates exclude projections of use of PRGF resources and HIPC assistance by Liberia, Somalia, and Sudan, which presently have protracted overdue financial obligations to the IMF.

TABLE IV.4. PRGF-HIPC TRUST: FINANCING REQUIREMENTS
AND SOURCES OF FINANCING, AS OF APRIL 30, 2001

	In Billions of SDRs (End-2000 NPV)
Total IMF financing requirements	3.0
PRGF subsidy requirement	1.1
Cost of the HIPC Initiative to the IMF	1.9
Sources of financing	3.0
Effective	
Bilateral contributions	1.1
IMF contributions	1.8
Investment income from gold proceeds	1.4
Other contributions	0.5
Pending	
Bilateral contributions	0.1

Bilateral pledges from member countries come from a wide spectrum of the IMF's membership, demonstrating the broad support for the HIPC and PRGF initiatives. In all, 94 member countries have pledged their support: 27 industrial countries, 58 developing countries, and 9 countries in transition. As of end-April 2001, effective bilateral contributions amounted to SDR 1.1 billion in NPV terms, or 93 percent of total pledged contributions.

The bulk of the IMF's contribution comes from the investment income on the net proceeds equivalent to SDR 1.4 billion in NPV terms generated from off-market transactions in gold of 12.9 million fine troy ounces. The off-market gold transactions were completed in April 2000, generating net proceeds of SDR 2.226 billion. These resources have been placed in the SDA and invested solely for the benefit of the HIPC Initiative. Transfers of the investment income on gold to the PRGF-HIPC Trust can only be made when all other available resources for the delivery of HIPC assistance have been exhausted (see the discussion of off-market gold transactions in Chapter II).

The IMF also contributes about SDR 0.5 billion in NPV terms by forgoing compensation for the administrative expenses related to PRGF operations for the financial years 1998 through 2004. The equivalent amount is transferred from the Reserve Account of the PRGF Trust to the PRGF-HIPC Trust. In addition, part of the interest surcharge on financing provided in 1998 and 1999 under the SRF related to activation of the NAB have also been transferred to the PRGF-HIPC Trust.[13]

At end-April 2001, the IMF had committed enhanced HIPC Initiative assistance of SDR 1.3 billion in NPV terms to 22 member countries that had reached decision points under the enhanced HIPC framework, one of which, Uganda, had reached the completion point.[14] Of this amount, SDR 0.5 billion in NPV terms was disbursed (Table IV.5). Since interim PRGF operations have not begun, no resources have been committed for interim PRGF subsidies.

To ensure the continuity of PRGF operations after existing loan resources in the PRGF Trust are fully committed, additional loan resources of SDR 4– 4½ billion need to be mobilized for an interim period until PRGF operations become self-sustained after 2005. As of end-April 2001, a number of member countries had indicated their readiness to provide new loans for this purpose.

Financial Statements of the PRGF-HIPC Trust

The sources and uses of resources under the PRGF-HIPC Trust are summarized in its balance sheet (Table IV.6) and income statement (Table IV.7), as discussed above for the PRGF Trust.

Operational Structure

When the PRGF-HIPC Trust was established in 1997, it was envisaged that financial contributions could be earmarked for either PRGF subsidies or HIPC Initiative assistance. To permit such earmarking, three separate subaccounts were established (Figure IV.4):

- the HIPC subaccount for resources earmarked for HIPC Initiative assistance;
- the PRGF subaccount for resources earmarked for interim PRGF subsidy operations; and
- the PRGF-HIPC subaccount for unearmarked resources.

---

[13]On April 28, 1999, the participants in the NAB unanimously decided that, as a condition for the activation of the NAB to finance purchases by Brazil, one-third of the surcharge on outstanding purchases made under the SRF by Brazil be transferred to the PRGF-HIPC Trust. As of end-April 2000, Brazil completed all NAB-financed SRF repurchases, which generated transfers of SDR 72.5 million in support of HIPC operations.

[14]As noted in Table IV.5, one additional country, Côte d'Ivoire, had resources committed under the original HIPC Initiative. On June 8, 2001, Bolivia also reached its completion point.

TABLE IV.5. HIPC ASSISTANCE BY THE IMF,
FINANCIAL YEAR ENDED APRIL 30, 2001
(In millions of SDRs)

Member[2]	Amount[1] Committed	Amount[1] Disbursed[3]
Benin	18.4	3.7
Bolivia	62.4	21.2
Burkina Faso	31.3	17.8
Cameroon	28.5	2.2
Côte d'Ivoire[4]	14.4	—
Gambia, The	1.8	0.1
Guinea	24.2	2.4
Guinea-Bissau	9.2	0.5
Guyana	56.2	31.7
Honduras	22.7	—
Madagascar	16.6	0.7
Malawi	23.1	2.3
Mali	44.4	11.5
Mauritania	34.8	9.9
Mozambique	104.8	95.5
Nicaragua	63.0	—
Niger	21.6	0.4
Rwanda	33.8	6.8
São Tomé and Príncipe	—	—
Senegal	33.8	4.8
Tanzania	89.0	26.7
Uganda	120.1	120.1
Zambia	468.8	117.2
Total	1,322.9	475.5

Note: Numbers may not add to totals due to rounding.

[1]Amounts may include interest on amounts committed but not disbursed during the interim period between the decision and completion points.

[2]Twenty-three members, of which 22 under the enhanced HIPC framework.

[3]These amounts are grants from the PRGF-HIPC Trust Account to member accounts to be used for repayments to the IMF as they fall due.

[4]Under the original HIPC framework.

Resources earmarked for the HIPC subaccount include investment income on the net proceeds derived from off-market gold transactions and certain bilateral contributions. Together these resources amount to SDR 1.7 billion

TABLE IV.6. PRGF-HIPC TRUST AND RELATED ACCOUNTS: COMBINED BALANCE SHEETS,
AS OF APRIL 30, 2001
(In millions of SDRs)

| | PRGF-HIPC Trust Account | | | | Umbrella Account for HIPC Operations | Post-SCA-2 Administered Account | Combined Total |
| | | Subaccount | | | | | |
	PRGF-HIPC	PRGF	HIPC	Combined			
Assets							
Cash and cash equivalents	536.9	6.4	3.9	547.2	304.4	92.1	943.7
Investments	444.1	7.5	—	451.7	35.0	—	486.7
Transfers receivable	12.5	—	—	12.5	—	—	12.5
Transfers to and from subaccounts	214.2	—	(214.2)	—	—	—	—
Interest receivable	5.3	0.1	0.1	5.5	4.0	1.2	10.7
Total assets	1,213.1	14.0	(210.3)	1,016.8	343.4	93.3	1,453.6
Resources and liabilities							
Borrowings	477.2	—	—	477.2	—	—	477.2
Interest payable	0.9	—	—	0.9	—	—	0.9
Total liabilities	478.0	—	—	478.0	—	—	478.0
Resources	735.1	14.0	(210.3)	538.8	343.4	93.3	975.5
Total resources and liabilities	1,213.1	14.0	(210.3)	1,016.8	343.4	93.3	1,453.6

Note: Numbers may not add to totals due to rounding.

137

TABLE IV.7. PRGF-HIPC TRUST AND RELATED ACCOUNTS: COMBINED INCOME STATEMENTS, FINANCIAL YEAR ENDED APRIL 30, 2001

(*In millions of SDRs*)

| | PRGF-HIPC Trust Account | | | | Umbrella Account for HIPC Operations | Post-SCA-2 Administered Account | Combined Total |
| | Subaccount | | | Combined | | | |
	PRGF-HIPC	PRGF	HIPC				
Balance, April 30, 2000	491.0	7.3	12.7	511.1	160.8	257.1	928.9
Investment income	52.7	0.6	5.6	45.3	11.2	7.9	64.3
Interest expense	(1.4)	—	(13.5)	(1.4)	—	—	(1.4)
Other expenses	(0.2)	—	—	(0.2)	—	—	(0.2)
Operational income (loss)	51.0	0.5	(7.9)	43.6	11.2	7.9	62.7
Contributions received	138.0	6.1	47.7	191.9	262.8	—	454.7
Grants	—	—	(262.8)	(262.8)	—	—	(262.8)
Disbursements	—	—	—	—	(91.4)	—	(91.4)
Net income (loss)	189.1	6.7	(223.0)	(27.2)	182.6	7.9	163.2
Transfers	55.0	—	—	55.0	—	(171.6)	(116.6)
Net changes in resources	244.1	6.7	(223.0)	27.8	182.6	(163.7)	46.6
Balance, April 30, 2001	735.1	14.0	(210.3)	538.8	343.4	93.3	975.5

Note: Numbers may not add to totals due to rounding.

FIGURE IV.4. FINANCIAL STRUCTURE OF THE PRGF-HIPC TRUST

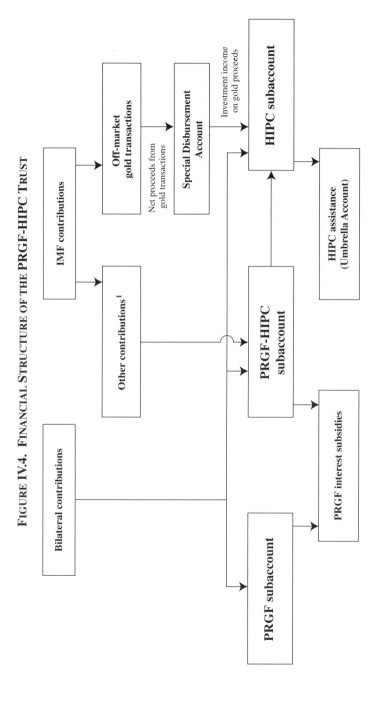

[1]Includes transfers equivalent to the cost of administering PRGF operations for FY1998–2004 and transfers of part of the interest surcharge on certain outstanding purchases under the Supplemental Reserve Facility.

in NPV terms, compared with the estimated HIPC Initiative financing requirement of SDR 1.9 billion in NPV terms. Since expected HIPC financing requirements exceed resources earmarked for the HIPC Initiative, and the investment income on the net proceeds derived from gold sales accrues only slowly over time, the structure of the PRGF-HIPC Trust allows the HIPC subaccount to borrow resources from the PRGF-HIPC subaccount for HIPC operations.

All HIPC Initiative assistance provided by the PRGF-HIPC Trust is disbursed from the HIPC subaccount to the beneficiaries. The investment earnings on resources generated from gold sales held in the SDA will be made available to the HIPC subaccount to meet the costs of the HIPC Initiative. As the HIPC subaccount is replenished over time, any borrowings from the PRGF-HIPC subaccount are to be repaid. To preserve the value of resources for the continuation of PRGF operations, the HIPC subaccount will pay interest on the temporary use of resources of the PRGF-HIPC subaccount at a rate equal to the average return on investment of SDA resources.

Self-Sustained PRGF

Following the interim PRGF, the IMF intends to continue to provide concessional lending to eligible members under PRGF-like arrangements. It is expected that both loan and subsidy resources for this purpose will be provided through a revolving use of the balances currently accumulating in the Reserve Account of the PRGF Trust.

New Investment Strategy

In March 2000, the IMF initiated a new investment strategy for the assets of the SDA and other resources of the PRGF and PRGF-HIPC Trusts with the objective of supplementing returns over time while maintaining prudent limits on risk. The supplemental income will be used to enhance the level of protection accorded to lenders to the PRGF Trust, provide an additional margin for subsidizing PRGF lending, generate additional subsidy and grant resources for interim PRGF and HIPC operations, and expand the size of the self-sustained PRGF.

Under the new approach, the maturity of SDA, PRGF, and PRGF-HIPC investments was lengthened by shifting the bulk of assets previously invested in short-term SDR-denominated deposits with the BIS to portfolios

---

BOX IV.4. INVESTMENT STRATEGY

At the core of the investment mandate given to external bond managers is the one- to three-year benchmark bond index, which embodies the IMF's baseline risk and return preferences for longer-term bond investments and is the neutral position toward which external bond managers are expected to gravitate. The bond benchmark is a customized index[1] comprising the Merrill Lynch one- to three-year government bond indices for Germany, Japan, the United Kingdom, and the United States with each market weighted to reflect the currency composition of the SDR basket.

The new strategy is implemented on the IMF's behalf by the BIS, the World Bank, and three private investment managers. Assets are actively managed and invested in domestic government bonds of the euro zone, Japan, the United Kingdom, and the United States, as well as bonds issued by eligible national and international financial organizations in SDRs or a currency included in the SDR basket. Managers are permitted to invest in eligible securities across the maturity spectrum, provided that the sensitivity of the portfolio to changes in market interest rates remains broadly in line with that of the benchmark index.

Investments may be made only in cash securities; positions in derivative securities are not permitted. There may be no short selling or any form of leverage. Foreign exchange risk is to be tightly controlled through regular portfolio rebalancing.

---

[1]In contrast, the MTI benchmark employs the J.P. Morgan one- to three-year government bond indices for Germany, Japan, the United Kingdom, and the United States, weighted to reflect the composition of the SDR basket.

---

of bonds and other medium-term instruments (MTIs)[15] structured to reflect the currency composition of the SDR basket (Box IV.4). Remaining short-term deposits are held at a level sufficient to meet liquidity requirements[16]

---

[15]MTIs perform similarly to domestic government bonds, but are claims on the BIS that offer ready liquidity and the possibility to benefit from a credit spread over domestic government bonds.

[16]Short-term deposits held to meet liquidity requirements are kept at a level sufficient to meet three-months' projected cash outflows for PRGF subsidies and HIPC grants, plus a margin for deposits that may be withdrawn by depositors in case of balance of payments need and for possible delays in the repayment of PRGF obligations.

and to conform with the administrative arrangements agreed with certain contributors.

In the first 12 months since its inception, the new investment strategy added about 220 basis points (on an annualized basis, net of fees) to returns over the previous approach of investing in SDR-denominated deposits — generating supplemental income of nearly SDR 140 million in support of PRGF and PRGF-HIPC operations.

V

Safeguards for IMF Assets

Article I(v) of the IMF Articles of Agreement specifies that one of the purposes of the IMF is "To give confidence to members by making the general resources of the Fund temporarily available to them *under adequate safeguards….*" Moreover, Article V, Section 3*(a)* requires the IMF to "adopt policies…that will *establish adequate safeguards* for the temporary use of the general resources of the Fund" (italics added).

The IMF has established safeguards to protect its currently available and outstanding credit. These safeguards cover six broad elements of IMF operations:

- limits on access to appropriate amounts of financing, with incentives to contain excessively long and heavy use;
- conditionality and program design;
- safeguards assessments of central banks;
- post-program monitoring;
- measures to deal with misreporting; and
- various voluntary services of the IMF, such as technical assistance; the transparency initiative, including the establishment and monitoring of codes and standards, particularly, monetary and fiscal transparency and the assessment of financial sector soundness; and the governance initiative.

The monetary character of the IMF, as well as the need for its resources to revolve, requires that members with financial obligations to the institution repay them as they fall due so that these resources can be made available to other members. Since the early 1980s, overdue obligations to the IMF have been a matter of serious concern because they weaken the IMF's liquidity position and impose a cost on other members. The direct cost of overdue obligations to members is reflected in higher charges for borrowers and in a lower rate of remuneration paid to creditors.

Safeguards put in place to deal with overdue obligations to the IMF include the following two broad areas:

- Policies to assist members in clearing arrears to the IMF, including:
  —the cooperative arrears strategy, consisting of three components: prevention of arrears, collaboration in clearing arrears, and remedial

measures, which are intended to have a deterrent effect for countries that do not cooperate actively; and
— the rights approach, which allows a member in arrears to accumulate "rights" to future disbursements from the IMF.
- Measures to protect the IMF's financial position.

The remainder of this chapter expands upon the role and content of these various safeguards for IMF resources.

Safeguarding Available and Outstanding Credit

Limiting Access and Providing Appropriate Incentives

The first safeguard to ensure the temporary and appropriate use of IMF resources is the IMF's policies regarding access under the credit tranches and various lending facilities in the GRA, and to its concessional assistance under the PRGF and PRGF-HIPC Trusts. Access policy in the GRA is discussed in Chapter II, along with the measures that have been adopted to discourage excessively large or prolonged use of IMF resources. To limit unduly large use of IMF resources, surcharges are imposed on credit outstanding above a threshold level. Prolonged use of IMF resources is addressed through time-based repurchase expectations, which come into force before the standard repurchase obligations (see Table II.2).

Access policies for concessional IMF assistance are discussed in Chapter IV.

Conditionality and Program Design

Once the level of access has been determined, conditionality is the next line of defense in safeguarding IMF resources. Conditionality comprises an evolving set of guidelines covering the economic policies that members intend to follow as a condition for the use of IMF resources. The key objective of conditionality is to ensure that members drawing on the IMF adopt adequate policies to cope with their balance of payments problems and enable them to repay the IMF within the designated repurchase period. At the same time, conditionality is designed to give confidence to members that IMF resources will continue to be available to them if the terms of the associated arrangement are met.

Conditionality operates through a number of instruments:
- Members formally request an arrangement with the IMF through a Letter of Intent. This document describes the economic program to be

supported by IMF resources and may be accompanied by a more detailed Memorandum of Economic and Financial Policies.

- All arrangements in the upper credit tranches and under the EFF feature phased purchases. This reflects the strong link that is established between IMF financing and policy adjustment. Most arrangements incorporate an even phasing of purchases, but where adjustment is concentrated at the beginning of an arrangement, purchases can be front-loaded.

- The second and any subsequent purchases after approval of the arrangement are normally contingent on the observance of performance criteria. These are intended to cover the crucial objectives of the adjustment program that are under the control of the authorities, such as management of international reserves, monetary policy, fiscal policy, external debt, and structural reforms where these are considered essential. All arrangements additionally include a number of standard performance clauses prohibiting the introduction or intensification of exchange and trade restrictions and the accumulation of external payments arrears.

- Some purchases under arrangements are conditional on completion of scheduled program reviews. These allow for the assessment of progress on policies that cannot easily be quantified or defined in performance criteria. If a program review is delayed and slips past a subsequent test date, the later performance criteria become applicable.

- A member may be expected to implement some corrective measures before an arrangement is approved, a program review is completed, or a waiver of a performance criterion is granted. These prior actions are specific measures whose implementation is both readily verifiable and subject to a realistic timetable.

The design of adjustment programs is critical in keeping an arrangement on track to meet performance criteria and complete program reviews. There is no single model of adjustment that is applied indiscriminately to all members; members design their own programs, in close consultation with IMF staff. All adjustment programs supported by the IMF nevertheless share a common objective: to achieve a current account position that is sustainable by normal capital flows without resort to restrictions that would be harmful to the member or other members.

Conditionality has evolved substantially over the years. Until the 1980s, policy conditions were primarily limited to macroeconomic variables, such as those related to domestic credit creation and the fiscal deficit. Starting in the late 1980s, however, there was a broadening of the scope of conditionality. In part, this reflected the increasing emphasis on growth as an objective of IMF-supported programs, together with the growing involvement of the IMF with members where severe structural problems were impeding the achievement of a sustainable balance of payments position. As a result, IMF conditionality expanded to encompass structural reforms, including those intended to strengthen fiscal institutions, build a sound financial sector, and increase the efficiency of the economy more generally.

The expansion of conditionality has raised a number of issues. In particular, it has created concerns that excessively broad and detailed conditionality may undermine national ownership of policy programs, which is essential for successful program implementation. Moreover, extensive conditionality may strain the member's administrative capacity, thus undermining implementation of those policies that are truly essential. The IMF is therefore in the midst of an effort to streamline and focus its conditionality. Pending the completion of that review, conditionality in new and existing IMF arrangements is subject to an "Interim Guidance Note on Streamlining Structural Conditionality."[1]

Safeguards Assessments of Central Banks

Background

In March 2000, the Executive Board adopted a strengthened framework of measures to safeguard the use of IMF resources through the introduction of safeguards assessments of central banks. The framework was developed in the wake of instances of misreporting and allegations of misuse of IMF resources. Revised guidelines on misreporting were put in place (see below), and safeguards assessments were adopted as an ex ante mechanism to help prevent the misreporting of information and possible misuse of IMF resources.

The specific objective of safeguards assessments is to provide reasonable assurance to the IMF that a central bank's control, accounting, reporting, and auditing systems in place to manage resources are adequate to ensure the integrity of operations. Central bank practices and procedures are reviewed because central banks are in most cases the recipients and guard-

---

[1]See "Interim Guidance Note on Streamlining Structural Conditionality" (http://www.imf.org/external/np/pdr/cond/2001/eng/091800.pdf).

ians of IMF disbursements to members in their roles as the member's fiscal agent and depository for the IMF.

Safeguards assessments apply to all members with arrangements for use of IMF resources approved after June 30, 2000. Member countries with arrangements in effect prior to June 30, 2000 are subject to transitional procedures. These countries are required to demonstrate the adequacy of only one key element of the safeguards framework, namely that their central banks publish annual financial statements that are audited by external auditors in accordance with internationally accepted standards.[2] The focus is on the external audit because it provides a foundation for the provision of reliable financial information, and is considered an essential component of a central bank's overall governance structure.

Conceptual Framework

Safeguards assessments consider the adequacy of five key areas of control and governance within a central bank (Box V.1). These five areas can be summarized under the acronym ELRIC, as follows:

- **E**xternal audit mechanism,
- **L**egal structure and independence,
- financial **R**eporting,
- **I**nternal audit mechanism, and
- system of internal **C**ontrols.

The ELRIC framework is derived from the IMF's "Code of Good Practices on Transparency in Monetary and Financial Polices" and employs International Accounting Standards (IAS), International Standards on Auditing (ISA), and the IMF's data dissemination standards (the Special Data Dissemination Standard (SDDS) and the General Data Dissemination System (GDDS)) as benchmarks (see below). In the area of the legal structure and independence, there is no generally accepted benchmark for central bank independence and legal structure. The framework, therefore, calls for the identification in the legislation governing the central bank of any provision that could allow for undue interference with central bank operations by outside parties, that could jeopardize the central bank's governance

---

[2]The term "external auditor" is used to distinguish the external audit of the financial statements from the activities of the internal audit department that is typically part of a central bank. The external auditor, usually an accounting firm or a supreme audit institution, is expected to be independent of the central bank.

Box V.1. Safeguards Assessments of Central Banks

The five key areas of the formal safeguards assessments framework are as follows:
- *External Audit Mechanism.* The external audit mechanism comprises the practices and procedures in place to enable an independent auditor to express an opinion as to whether the financial statements are prepared, in all material respects, in accordance with an established financial reporting framework. An external audit mechanism is important for the credibility of a central bank; the objective of the assessment is to establish whether an independent and high-quality external audit of the central bank's financial statements is conducted regularly and whether previous recommendations made by the auditors have been implemented. The assessment also ascertains whether an audit opinion is published with the financial statements.
- *The Legal Structure and Independence.* Government interference with central bank operations can undermine a central bank's autonomy and increase the risks to which it is exposed, particularly if agencies other than the central bank have responsibility for reserves management. The objective in assessing this area is to ensure that (1) the arrangements whereby the central bank extends credits, advances, or overdrafts to the government follow legal procedures, and that the government has not interfered with these regulations; and (2) for those agencies that share monetary authority with the central bank, the legal basis of their relationship to the central bank, their role as a monetary authority, and the responsibility for reserves management are transparent and explicit.
- *Financial Reporting.* Adequate financial reporting practices are an essential element of effective central bank operations and encompass the provision of both internal information (including financial, operational, and compliance data) and external market information about events and conditions that support decision making. For such information to be useful it must be relevant, reliable, timely, accessible, and provided in a consistent format. The objective in assessing financial reporting practices is to ensure that the central bank adheres to international good practices in its accounting principles, financial statement presentation and disclosures, coverage of operations, and reporting of statistical data. Nonadherence to accepted good practices might be an indicator of a lack of transparency and accountability.
- *Internal Audit Mechanism.* Internal auditing is an independent, objective assurance and consulting activity designed to add value and improve an organization's operations. It helps an organization accomplish its objectives by bringing a systematic, disciplined approach to evaluating and improving the effectiveness of its risk management, control, and governance processes. The objective in assessing the internal audit function at a central bank is to evaluate its effectiveness by considering the organizational independence and objectivity that allows

the internal audit activity to fulfill the nature and scope of its work program and the procedures for communicating results unencumbered from external interference.

- *System of Internal Controls.* Internal control is a process comprising all the policies and procedures effected by the board, management, and other personnel of a central bank to assist in achieving (1) the effective and efficient conduct of its business; (2) its compliance with applicable laws, regulations, policies, plans, and internal rules and procedures; and (3) the timely preparation of reliable financial information. A system of effective internal controls is a critical component for the sound operation of central bank activities, including the safeguarding of assets, the prevention and detection of fraud and error, and the accuracy and completeness of accounting records. The objective in assessing internal control systems is to determine whether appropriate procedures are in place, at all levels, to provide reasonable assurance that material risks that could adversely affect the central bank's operations are being continuously recognized, assessed, and mitigated. The main focus is on controls over the banking, accounting, and foreign exchange operations of the central bank.

structure in any way, or that gives monetary or reserves management authority to an entity other than the central bank.

In order to ensure a reasonable degree of consistency across countries, IMF staff has developed standardized analytical techniques and assessment tools for each element of ELRIC. At the same time, in applying the benchmarks, due consideration is given to the country's degree of economic development and to its central bank's complexity of operations. Such flexibility in the assessment framework is considered necessary to allow for a variety of appropriate remedial actions, ranging from long-term technical assistance to the possibility of prior actions before further disbursements by the IMF.

Modalities

The IMF Treasurer's Department takes the lead in implementing safeguards assessments, which are undertaken in two stages:

Stage One is a preliminary assessment of the adequacy of the central bank's ELRIC based on a review of documentation provided by the authorities and, if necessary, discussions with the external auditors. Vulnerabilities identified during a Stage One assessment are documented, together with judgment about whether or not a Stage Two on-site assessment is necessary.

In cases where a Stage Two assessment is not considered necessary, but vulnerabilities are nonetheless identified, the staff recommends remedial actions that, if endorsed by management, are discussed with country authorities and presented to the Executive Board in conjunction with other IMF program issues.

Stage Two on-site assessment missions confirm or modify the preliminary conclusions drawn by the Stage One assessment and propose specific remedial measures to alleviate confirmed vulnerabilities in a central bank's ELRIC. The remedial actions are discussed with central bank officials and incorporated into the member's program of reforms.

The modalities for transitional procedures that are applicable to countries with IMF arrangements in effect prior to June 30, 2000 are similar to a Stage One assessment. Central banks whose financial statements are presently not audited by external auditors are expected to commit at the next program review to implement an acceptable external audit mechanism under an agreed-upon timetable. For central banks that have an external audit mechanism and vulnerabilities are identified, staff recommends specific remedial actions in the same manner as for Stage One assessments.

Post-Program Monitoring

While the above safeguards focus on the identification and reduction of risks before or during the disbursement of IMF resources, post-program monitoring takes place after the disbursement phase. Post-program monitoring provides for closer monitoring of the circumstances and policies of members that have substantial IMF credit outstanding following the expiration of their IMF arrangements. Introduced in 2000 during the review of IMF facilities, post-program monitoring formalizes the long-standing consultation provisions included in all IMF arrangements. A guidance note on the implementation of post-program monitoring is available on the IMF's website.[3]

The aim of post-program monitoring is to identify and address risks at an early stage. Such monitoring is intended to provide an early warning of policies that could call into question a member's continued progress toward external viability, and thus could eventually imperil IMF resources. It also serves as a mechanism for bringing these issues to the attention of the authorities and the Executive Board and for stimulating action to improve the situa-

---

[3]"Review of Fund Facilities: Proposed Decisions and Implementation Guidelines" (November 2, 2000). See http://www.imf.org/external/np/pdr/fac/2000/02/index.htm.

tion. A Public Information Notice (PIN) and the associated staff report are published on a voluntary basis following Executive Board consideration.

Measures to Deal with Misreporting

Background

The IMF needs reliable information for every aspect of its work, and it is particularly important in ensuring that its resources are used for their intended purposes. While known incidents of misreporting and misuse of the IMF's resources have been rare, it is important to the integrity of the IMF's reputation as a prudent provider of financial assistance to respond quickly and effectively to any allegations of misreporting or misuse of its resources. Unlike project-related loans, IMF disbursements are typically added to a country's gross international reserves for general use by the country. As a result, the fungibility of resources, both domestic and foreign, makes it extremely difficult, if not impossible, to track the specific uses of reserves.

The term misreporting is used broadly to cover situations in which a member provides incorrect information to the IMF. It is often difficult to establish the reason why information was misreported, but several factors have arisen, including administrative lapses, weaknesses in statistical capacity, inherent subjectivity of certain data, negligence, and deliberate misrepresentation.

The IMF has developed a set of guidelines or rules that govern misreporting in the context of a member's provision of information under an IMF-supported economic program. The guidelines apply whenever a member makes a purchase or receives a disbursement from the IMF on the basis of inaccurate information. The guidelines cover all IMF lending facilities, including emergency assistance and the CFF, but not HIPC assistance at present. The guidelines apply regardless of the reason for misreporting and establish a limitation period of four years over which the IMF can take action.

Misreporting can also arise under the IMF's Articles in the context of the general obligation of all members, irrespective of whether or not they have used IMF resources, to provide the IMF with relevant economic information. Article VIII, Section 5 specifies members' continuing obligation to provide the IMF with the information the IMF deems necessary for its activities. In addition to the specific data listed in the Articles, members are also required to provide any additional information requested by the Managing Director or required in Executive Board decisions. Members must provide all information "in as detailed and accurate a manner as is practicable and, so far as possible, to avoid mere estimates."

151

Procedures and Remedies

Whenever evidence indicates that misreporting may have occurred, the Managing Director consults with the member and submits a report to the Executive Board together with a recommendation for the course of action to be taken by the Board. A member found to have breached Article VIII, Section 5 may be subject to the remedial measures specified in the Articles for a breach of obligation, including the possibility of a declaration of ineligibility to draw on IMF resources. In determining whether a member has breached its obligations under Article VIII, Section 5, the Executive Board must take into account the member's capacity to produce the relevant information.

Under the misreporting guidelines, a member found to have obtained the use of IMF resources on the basis of information that proves to be incorrect is deemed to have made a noncomplying purchase. The member is required to repay the IMF, normally within 30 days, unless the Executive Board grants a waiver. Waivers can be granted if the deviations are minor or temporary, or the member has taken additional policy measures appropriate to achieve the objectives of the economic program. Failure to meet the repayment expectation will result in suspension of further purchases or disbursements under an existing arrangement and could trigger action to declare the member ineligible to draw on IMF resources. Interest may be charged on the amount subject to repayment expectation at the rate applicable to overdue amounts.

Publication of Misreporting Cases

After the Executive Board has made its determination about misreporting, the IMF makes public relevant information for each case of misreporting. Publication is automatic, but reviewed by the Executive Board on a case-by-case basis. The public statement is appropriately calibrated to the circumstances of the case and takes into account the seriousness of the misreporting, remedial measures taken, and other relevant considerations.

Voluntary Safeguards

The main objective of IMF technical assistance is to contribute to the development of the productive resources of member countries by enhancing the effectiveness of economic policy and financial management.[4] The IMF seeks to achieve this objective in two ways:

---

[4]For more information, see "Policy Statement on IMF Technical Assistance," issued on April 1, 2001 (see http://www.imf.org/external/pubs/ft/psta/index.htm).

- by supporting the efforts of members to strengthen their capacity—in both human and institutional resources—to formulate and implement sustainable, growth-oriented, and poverty-reducing macroeconomic, financial, and structural policies; and
- by assisting countries in the design of appropriate macroeconomic and structural policy reforms, taking account of the lessons learned by other countries in addressing similar economic policy reforms.

As the IMF seeks to strengthen recipient country ownership, its technical assistance program is based on the fundamental principle that to be effective and to have a high impact, it is important to ensure that a partner country is fully committed to owning the work associated with the assistance and implementing the recommendations flowing from the technical assistance.

Regarding other voluntary safeguards, the IMF has responded to calls for increased transparency for all members through a number of initiatives on the interrelated issues of codes and best practices. These initiatives are part of the broader effort to improve the architecture of the international financial system. The concept of internationally agreed standards is not new: for many years standards have provided a context within which policy advice and technical assistance have been provided to national authorities. The IMF, along with other multilateral institutions, has launched a series of transparency initiatives focusing on assessments of four main internationally recognized standards. These are:[5]

- the Special Data Dissemination Standard (SDDS),
- the Basel Core Principles,

---

[5]The SDDS (http://www.dsbb.imf.org/sddsindex.htm) is a standard of good practices in the dissemination of economic and financial data to which IMF member countries may subscribe on a voluntary basis. It is intended for use mainly by countries that either have or seek access to international financial markets, to signal their commitment to the provision of timely and comprehensive data. The "Basel Core Principles for Effective Banking Supervision" (http://www.bis.org) are intended to serve as a basic reference for supervisory and other public authorities within their jurisdictions. "The Code of Good Practices on Fiscal Transparency" (http://www.imf.org/external/np/fad/trans/code.htm) aims at leading to a better-informed public debate about the design and results of fiscal policy, making governments more accountable for the implementation of fiscal policy, and thereby strengthening credibility and public understanding of macroeconomic policies and choices. The "Code of Good Practices on Transparency in Monetary and Financial Policies" (http://www.imf.org/external/np/mae/mft/index.htm) is a guide for members to assess the degree of transparency in their institutional and operational frameworks for monetary and financial policies.

- the fiscal transparency code, and
- the monetary and financial transparency code.

The SDDS, principles, and codes are generally accepted as benchmarks of good practices on a voluntary basis. The IMF and World Bank have collaborated closely to assess progress in implementing selected standards. These summary assessments are referred to as "Reports on the Observance of Standards and Codes" (ROSCs), and a large number of them have been posted on the IMF's website on a voluntary basis by the member countries involved. In this context, the joint IMF–World Bank Financial Sector Assessment Program (FSAP) has undertaken a number of assessments of the stability of countries' financial system.[6] More recently, the IMF has also been addressing issues of best practice in the related areas of foreign reserves management and the development of macroprudential indicators.[7]

In 1997, following a discussion on the role of the IMF in governance issues, the IMF Executive Board approved a "Guidance Note on Governance."[8] The note was prepared in recognition of the importance of good governance for macroeconomic stability and sustained noninflationary growth, the promotion of which forms part of the IMF's mandate. Its central message was a call for greater attention by the IMF to issues of governance, in particular through:

- a more comprehensive treatment in the context of both Article IV consultations and IMF-supported programs of those governance issues that are within the IMF's mandate and expertise;
- a more proactive approach in advocating policies and the development of institutions and administrative systems that eliminate the opportunity for rent-seeking, corruption, and fraudulent activity in the management of public resources;
- an evenhanded treatment of governance issues in all member countries; and
- enhanced collaboration with other multilateral institutions, in particular the World Bank, to make better use of complementary areas of expertise.

---

[6]The Financial System Stability Assessments under the FSAP reflect the Monetary and Financial Transparency Code and address systemic vulnerability issues in the financial system (http://www.imf.org/external/np/fsap).

[7]See IMF and World Bank, "Assessing the Implementation of Standards: A Review of Experience and Next Steps," January 11, 2001 (http://www.imf.org/external/np/pdr/sac/2001/eng/review.htm).

[8]See "The Role of the Fund in Governance Issues—Guidance Note," July 27, 1997 (http://www.imf.org/external/np/sec/nb/1997/nb9715.htm).

In cases where a governance issue with a macroeconomic impact lies outside the IMF's primary responsibilities, the IMF collaborates with other multilateral organizations possessing the appropriate expertise. In February 2001, the Executive Board reviewed the experience to date with the IMF's role in governance issues.[9]

Dealing with Overdue Financial Obligations

Overview

The IMF's experience with the timeliness of members in meeting their financial obligations was from the outset generally satisfactory. However, beginning in the early 1980s, partly because of the sharp increase in international interest rates, late payments to the IMF rose significantly in both frequency and amount. While most delays were corrected within a short period of time, the emergence of more protracted arrears raised serious concern and highlighted the need to develop more systematic procedures for dealing with arrears.

In the late 1980s and the early 1990s, the IMF strengthened its procedures for dealing with overdue obligations by adopting various measures, including IMF-monitored programs and informal staff monitoring—neither with financing—and the rights approach to help members in arrears establish a track record of cooperation with the IMF and eventually clear their arrears to the IMF. This process culminated in the adoption of the three-pronged cooperative strategy for handling arrears that emphasizes prevention of arrears, collaboration in clearing arrears, and remedial measures against continuing arrears in cases where active cooperation is lacking. The rights approach to arrears clearance is an integral part of the cooperative strategy.

The cooperative strategy has been broadly successful in preventing new cases of protracted arrears (defined as arrears outstanding for more than six months) from emerging and helping to resolve the cases of long-overdue payments that existed at end of the 1980s.[10] Of the 11 cases of protracted arrears at end-1989, 8 had been resolved by the mid-1990s, and only 3 new cases of protracted arrears emerged during the 1990s. At end-April 2001, of the 6

---

[9]See "Review of the Fund's Experience in Governance Issues," March 28, 2001 (http://www.imf.org/external/np/gov/2001/eng/report.htm).

[10]As the arrears strategy was strengthened in 1989, the current strategy is often called the strengthened cooperative strategy.

countries with protracted arrears to the IMF, most have experienced, or continue to experience, domestic conflicts, or international sanctions, or both.[11]

The level of outstanding arrears to the IMF has also declined over the last decade, from SDR 3.1 billion at end-1989 to SDR 2.2 billion at end-April 2001 (Figure V.1 and Figure V. 2). More than 80 percent of the arrears at end-April 2001 were obligations due to the GRA, with the balance due to the SDR Department, the Trust Fund, and SAF, all about evenly divided between overdue principal and overdue charges and interest payments. Arrears of the Democratic Republic of the Congo, Liberia, Somalia, and Sudan accounted for more than 95 percent of total overdue financial obligations to the IMF (Table V.1).

The Cooperative Strategy

Prevention

Prevention is the IMF's primary safeguard against the emergence of new cases of arrears, as discussed earlier. Preventive measures include IMF surveillance of members' economic policies, policy conditionality attached to the use of IMF resources, technical assistance by the IMF in support of members' adjustment and reform efforts, and the assurance of adequate balance of payments financing for members under IMF-supported programs.

In addition, the IMF has strengthened surveillance with the aim of improving its ability to identify emerging economic and financial difficulties in member countries. While these measures to strengthen the international financial architecture are not part of the IMF's cooperative strategy on arrears, they do have an indirect effect of limiting the need for IMF resources and thereby the emergence of arrears. In this area, greater attention has been given to members' timely provision of key economic and financial information, and a discussion of data availability and quality is required in relevant country reports. In view of the importance of the soundness of the banking system, the IMF has also taken steps to strengthen financial sector surveillance, focusing on members' financial and external vulnerability to crises. These efforts have been supplemented by debt sustainability analyses in cases of heavily indebted members, which identify the need for adjustment policies, debt relief, and other exceptional financial

---

[11]The Islamic State of Afghanistan, the Democratic Republic of the Congo, Iraq, Liberia, Somalia, and Sudan.

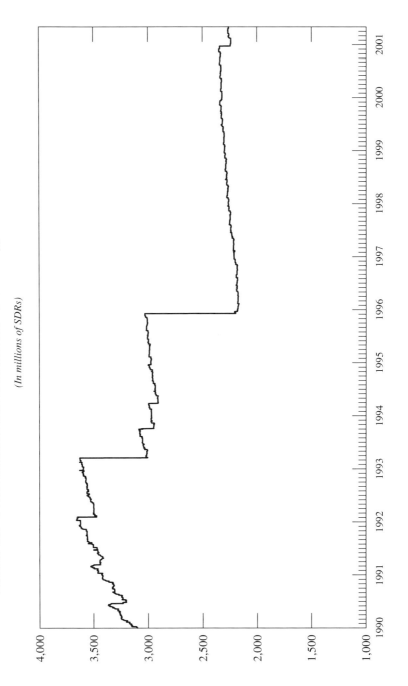

FIGURE V.1. OVERDUE FINANCIAL OBLIGATIONS TO THE IMF, JANUARY 1990–APRIL 2001

(*In millions of SDRs*)

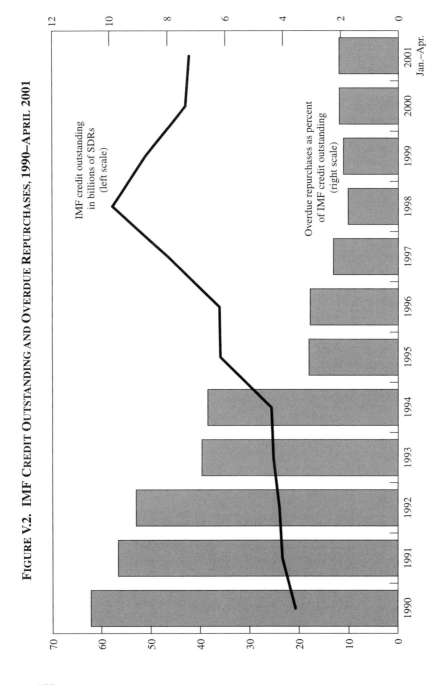

FIGURE V.2. IMF CREDIT OUTSTANDING AND OVERDUE REPURCHASES, 1990–APRIL 2001

IMF credit outstanding
in billions of SDRs
(left scale)

Overdue repurchases as percent
of IMF credit outstanding
(right scale)

TABLE V.1. ARREARS TO THE IMF OF COUNTRIES WITH OBLIGATIONS OVERDUE FOR SIX MONTHS OR MORE, BY TYPE AND DURATION, AS OF APRIL 30, 2001

(In millions of SDRs)

	Total	By Type			By Duration			
		General Department (Including SAF)	SDR Department	Trust Fund	Less than one year	1–2 years	2–3 years	3 years or more
Afghanistan, Islamic State of	6.2	—	6.2	—	1.4	1.1	1.2	2.5
Congo, Democratic Republic of the	391.8	375.7	16.1	—	13.3	19.2	27.8	331.5
Iraq	45.9	—	45.9	—	5.0	3.8	4.2	33.0
Liberia	484.8	433.5	21.2	30.1	12.8	9.7	10.6	451.7
Somalia	209.6	193.1	8.7	7.8	6.2	4.7	5.2	193.5
Sudan	1,103.2	1,025.1	0.1	78.0	23.7	19.5	22.9	1,037.0
Total	2,241.5	2,027.4	98.2	115.9	62.4	58.0	71.9	2,049.2

Note: Numbers may not add to totals due to rounding.

assistance to help achieve sustainable economic growth and durable poverty reduction.

Collaboration

The collaborative element of the arrears strategy provides a framework for cooperating members in arrears to establish a strong track record of policy performance and payments to the IMF and, in turn, to mobilize bilateral and multilateral financial support for their adjustment efforts and to clear arrears to the IMF and other creditors. Pursuit of the collaborative approach, including the use of the rights approach, has played an important role in resolving the protracted arrears of a number of members and contributed to the improved policy and payments performance in some of the current protracted arrears cases.

Established in 1990, the rights approach permits a member to establish a track record on policies and payments to the IMF under a rights accumulation program (RAP) and to earn "rights" to obtain IMF resources under successor arrangements following the completion of the program and settlement of the arrears to the IMF. Eligibility for the rights approach is limited to the 11 members in protracted arrears to the IMF at the end of 1989.[12] The rights approach facilitated the clearance of arrears and normalization of financial relations with Peru (1993), Sierra Leone (1994), and Zambia (1995), and remains available to Liberia, Somalia, and Sudan.[13]

Programs supported by the rights approach involve upper credit tranche conditionality and require modified financing assurances.[14] Under these programs, members are expected to adopt and implement strong adjustment programs that establish a credible track record of policy implementation and help create the conditions for sustained growth and substantial progress toward

---

[12]These were Cambodia, Guyana, Honduras, Liberia, Panama, Peru, Sierra Leone, Somalia, Sudan, Vietnam, and Zambia.

[13]To provide reassurance to lenders to the PRGF Trust that they would be repaid for PRGF (formerly ESAF) loans made to encash rights under the RAP, the IMF in 1993 pledged to sell up to 3 million ounces of gold if it were determined that the PRGF Reserve Account, plus other available means of financing, were insufficient to meet payments due to creditors. For a discussion of the gold pledge, see Chapter II.

[14]Financing assurances were modified from the usual IMF arrangements in the sense that arrears to the IMF (and possibly other multilateral institutions) could continue to be outstanding during the program period, although it is expected that the member will make maximum efforts to reduce its overdue obligations to the IMF.

external viability. Such programs should adhere to the macroeconomic and structural policy standards associated with programs supported under the EFF or PRGF. To support the member's adjustment efforts, adequate external financing is required for the program, including debt rescheduling and relief from bilateral and private creditors and new financing from various sources. Under rights accumulation programs (RAPs), members are expected, at a minimum, to remain current with the IMF and the World Bank on obligations falling due during the period of the program. RAPs are normally of a three-year duration, although flexibility to tailor the length of the agreed track record to the member's specific circumstances can be provided.[15]

As part of the collaborative approach, the IMF has also developed other measures, including IMF- and staff-monitored programs to help members in arrears establish a track record on policies and payments leading to eventual clearance of arrears to the IMF. These programs, supported by the provision of technical assistance from the IMF, have been instrumental in assisting these members in the design and implementation of appropriate economic policies and making progress toward normalization of financial relations with external creditors, including the IMF.

Over the past several years, the IMF's Executive Board has discussed on a number of occasions IMF assistance to post-conflict countries, including those with protracted arrears to the IMF.[16] Executive Directors noted the special challenges posed by the presence of large protracted arrears in these countries, and agreed that the IMF's arrears strategy provides adequate flexibility to address effectively the range of circumstances in these countries. To ensure a well-coordinated response to the special problems associated with arrears clearance, Executive Directors agreed that World Bank and IMF staff would prepare an arrears clearance plan with the member, in consultation with each other and other major creditors, once a post-conflict country with arrears had made adequate progress in restoring macroeconomic stability and re-establishing relations with the international community. Executive Directors also agreed that the IMF should consider relaxing its calls for payments to the IMF as a test of cooperation in post-conflict cases, provided the

---

[15]The length of the RAPs of the three countries that have made use of the rights approach was 1½ years for Peru, 1¾ years for Sierra Leone, and 3 years for Zambia.

[16]For a general discussion of post-conflict assistance beyond the arrears context, see Chapter II.

BOX V.2. MEASURES FOR DETERRENCE OF OVERDUE FINANCIAL OBLIGATIONS TO THE IMF: TIMETABLE OF PROCEDURES

Time After Emergence of Arrears	Action
Immediately	• Staff sends a cable urging the member to make payment promptly; this communication is followed up through the office of the concerned Executive Director.
	• The member is not permitted any use of the IMF's resources nor is any request for the use of IMF resources placed before the Executive Board until the arrears are cleared.
2 weeks	• Management sends a communication to the Governor for the member stressing the seriousness of the failure to meet obligations and urging full and prompt settlement.
1 month	• The Managing Director notifies the Executive Board that an obligation is overdue.
6 weeks	• The Managing Director notifies the member that unless the overdue obligations are settled promptly a complaint will be issued to the Executive Board.
	• The Managing Director consults with and recommends to the Executive Board that a communication concerning the member's situation be sent to selected IMF Governors or to all IMF Governors in the event that the member has not improved its cooperation with the IMF.
2 months	• A complaint regarding the member's overdue obligations is issued by the Managing Director to the Executive Board.
3 months	• The complaint is given substantive consideration by the Executive Board. The Board has usually decided to limit the member's use of the IMF's general resources and if overdue SDR obligations are involved, suspend its right to use SDRs.

6–12 months	• The Executive Board reviews its decision on limitation within 3 months, with the possibility of a second review if warranted.
	• Depending on the Executive Board's assessment of the specific circumstances and of the efforts being made by the member, a declaration of ineligibility is considered to take effect within 12 months after the emergence of arrears.
	• Communications are sent to all IMF Governors and the heads of selected international financial institutions regarding the member's continued failure to fulfill its financial obligations to the IMF at the same time as the declaration of ineligibility is considered.
Up to 15 months	• A declaration of noncooperation is considered within 3 months after the dispatch of the preceding communications.
Up to 18 months	• A decision on suspension of voting and representation rights is considered within 3 months after a declaration of noncooperation.
Up to 24 months	• The procedure on compulsory withdrawal is initiated within 6 months after a decision on suspension.

member is judged to be cooperating on policies and that all other multilateral creditors take comparable action.

Remedial Measures

Remedial measures, which are essentially sanctions, are the final component of the arrears strategy applied to member countries with overdue obligations that do not actively cooperate with the IMF in seeking a solution to their arrears problems, under an escalating time schedule (Box V.2 above)

This timetable guides Executive Board consideration of sanctions of increasing intensity, although the application of each particular step is considered in light of the individual circumstances of the member concerned. In cases where civil conflicts, the absence of a functioning government, or international sanctions have prevented the IMF from reaching a judgment regarding the member's cooperation, the application of these measures has been delayed or suspended until such a judgment can be reached.

A number of remedial measures have been applied against countries that remain in protracted arrears to the IMF. As of end-2000, the Islamic State of Afghanistan, the Democratic Republic of the Congo, Iraq, Liberia, Somalia, and Sudan remained ineligible to use the general resources of the IMF. Declarations of noncooperation were in effect for the Democratic Republic of the Congo (issued on February 14, 1992) and Liberia (issued on March 30, 1990). In addition, the voting rights of the Democratic Republic of the Congo remained suspended (effective June 2, 1994).

To further strengthen incentives for members in protracted arrears to cooperate with the IMF in solving their arrears problems, the Executive Board in 1999 established understandings regarding the de-escalation of remedial measures. The de-escalation process recognizes the efforts of a member to strengthen economic policies and establish a solid record of policy performance and payments to the IMF, with the ultimate objective of full clearance of arrears to the IMF. Under this process, the suspension of Sudan's voting rights in the IMF put in place in August 1993 was lifted in August 2000.

Protecting the IMF's Financial Position

Historically, the IMF accumulated reserves to protect against the risk of administrative deficits and capital loss. When overdue financial obligations became significant in the early 1980s, the IMF's income began to be affected. To avoid an overstatement of actual income, the Executive Board decided in March 1985 that charges due but not settled from members in arrears to the IMF for six months or more were to be reported as deferred, rather than current, income. Since that time, charges accrued from those members and not paid are excluded from income unless the member becomes current in paying its charges. Since May 1986, the financial consequences of overdue obligations to the IMF have, to the extent possible, been shared equally between debtor and creditor member countries (see Chapter II, Box II.9). Under the burden-sharing mechanism, the rate of charge is increased and the rate of remuneration reduced to generate suffi-cient resources to offset the income lost through the deferral of charges.[17] When deferred charges are settled by members clearing protracted arrears, equivalent amounts are distributed to members that previously paid higher charges or received reduced remuneration.

The IMF levies special charges on overdue repurchases or repayments. For overdue obligations to the GRA, special charges apply only to arrears of less than six months duration.[18] The special rate of charge on overdue repur-chases is set equal to the positive margin between the SDR interest rate and the basic rate of charge. As the basic rate of charge has exceeded the SDR interest rate since May 1993, this margin has been zero and the normal rate of charge has been levied on overdue repurchases. The special charge on overdue charges, levied for six months in the GRA, is set equal to the SDR interest rate.[19] Overdue repayments or interest to the PRGF Trust are charged interest at the SDR interest rate instead of the usual concessional rate of ½ of 1 percent on PRGF loans.[20]

---

[17]There are, however, limits on the potential adjustment to the rate of remuneration. The average rate of remuneration for an adjustment period cannot be reduced to less than 85 percent of the SDR interest rate for the purpose of generating resources to offset deferred charges and contributing to the SCA-1, unless the Executive Board so decides. In any case, under the IMF's Articles the rate of remuneration cannot fall to less than 80 percent of the SDR interest rate.

[18]Special charges are limited to members with arrears of less than six months because it is thought that, while these charges may provide an incentive to settle obligations due, in the long run they may add to the problem of members' overdue obligations, making even-tual arrears clearance more difficult. The same considerations lie behind the decision not to levy any special charges on charges overdue for six months or longer.

[19]The short duration of the levy of special charges on overdue charges significantly reduces interest compounding on overdue obligations.

[20]Overdue SAF and ESAF obligations are charged interest at the SDR interest rate less ½ of 1 percent, divided by two.

Appendix I

IMF MEMBERSHIP, QUOTAS, AND ALLOCATIONS OF SDRs,
AS OF APRIL 30, 2001

(In millions of SDRs and percent)

Member	Quota	Quota Share	Existing SDR Cumulative Allocation	Proposed Special SDR Allocation[1]
Afghanistan, I.S. of *	120.4	0.06	26.7	8.6
Albania	48.7	0.02	—	10.3
Algeria	1,254.7	0.59	128.6	139.4
Angola	286.3	0.13	—	60.8
Antigua and Barbuda	13.5	0.01	—	2.5
Argentina	2,117.1	1.00	318.4	132.2
Armenia	92.0	0.04	—	19.8
Australia	3,236.4	1.52	470.5	213.5
Austria	1,872.3	0.88	179.0	169.3
Azerbaijan	160.9	0.08	—	34.3
Bahamas, The	130.3	0.06	10.2	17.6
Bahrain	135.0	0.06	6.2	18.1
Bangladesh	533.3	0.25	47.1	67.9
Barbados	67.5	0.03	8.0	6.3
Belarus	386.4	0.18	—	82.2
Belgium	4,605.2	2.17	485.2	424.2
Belize	18.8	0.01	—	4.0
Benin	61.9	0.03	9.4	3.9
Bhutan	6.3	0.00	—	1.3
Bolivia	171.5	0.08	26.7	10.3
Bosnia and Herzegovina	169.1	0.08	20.5	15.0
Botswana	63.0	0.03	4.4	6.4
Brazil	3,036.1	1.43	358.7	277.7
Brunei Darussalam	150.0	0.07	—	44.0
Bulgaria	640.2	0.30	—	136.3
Burkina Faso	60.2	0.03	9.4	3.5
Burundi	77.0	0.04	13.7	3.1
Cambodia	87.5	0.04	15.4	3.6
Cameroon	185.7	0.09	24.5	15.1
Canada	6,369.2	3.00	779.3	487.2

IMF MEMBERSHIP, QUOTAS, AND ALLOCATIONS OF SDRS *(continued)*

Member	Quota	Quota Share	Existing SDR Cumulative Allocation	Proposed Special SDR Allocation[1]
Cape Verde	9.6	0.01	0.6	1.4
Central African Rep.	55.7	0.03	9.3	2.8
Chad	56.0	0.03	9.4	2.7
Chile	856.1	0.40	121.9	60.3
China	6,369.2	3.00	236.8	755.6
Colombia	774.0	0.36	114.3	50.3
Comoros	8.9	0.00	0.7	1.2
Congo, Dem. Rep. of *	291.0	0.14	86.3	29.4
Congo, Rep. of	84.6	0.04	9.7	7.3
Costa Rica	164.1	0.08	23.7	11.2
Côte d'Ivoire	325.2	0.15	37.8	32.0
Croatia	365.1	0.17	44.2	32.5
Cyprus	139.6	0.07	19.4	9.9
Czech Republic	819.3	0.39	—	172.8
Denmark	1,642.8	0.77	178.9	134.8
Djibouti	15.9	0.01	1.2	2.2
Dominica	8.2	0.00	0.6	1.2
Dominican Republic	218.9	0.10	31.6	15.0
Ecuador	302.3	0.14	32.9	31.3
Egypt	943.7	0.44	135.9	63.0
El Salvador	171.3	0.08	25.0	11.8
Equatorial Guinea	32.6	0.02	5.8	1.3
Eritrea	15.9	0.01	—	3.4
Estonia	65.2	0.03	—	13.6
Ethiopia	133.7	0.06	11.2	17.7
Fiji	70.3	0.03	7.0	8.0
Finland	1,263.8	0.60	142.7	110.0
France	10,738.5	5.06	1,079.9	1,093.8
Gabon	154.3	0.07	14.1	18.2
Gambia, The	31.1	0.01	5.1	1.6
Georgia	150.3	0.07	—	32.5
Germany	13,008.2	6.12	1,210.8	1,205.3
Ghana	369.0	0.17	63.0	17.3
Greece	823.0	0.39	103.5	68.7
Grenada	11.7	0.01	0.9	1.6

IMF MEMBERSHIP, QUOTAS, AND ALLOCATIONS OF SDRs *(continued)*

Member	Quota	Quota Share	Existing SDR Cumulative Allocation	Proposed Special SDR Allocation[1]
Guatemala	210.2	0.10	27.7	17.4
Guinea	107.1	0.05	17.6	5.5
Guinea-Bissau	14.2	0.01	1.2	1.9
Guyana	90.9	0.04	14.5	5.2
Haiti	60.7	0.03	13.7	4.1
Honduras	129.5	0.06	19.1	8.8
Hungary	1,038.4	0.49	—	221.3
Iceland	117.6	0.06	16.4	8.6
India	4,158.2	1.96	681.2	214.6
Indonesia	2,079.3	0.98	239.0	200.1
Iran, I. R. of	1,497.2	0.70	244.1	72.1
Iraq*	504.0	0.24	68.5	185.1
Ireland	838.4	0.39	87.3	66.6
Israel	928.2	0.44	106.4	88.9
Italy	7,055.5	3.32	702.4	643.4
Jamaica	273.5	0.13	40.6	18.3
Japan	13,312.8	6.27	891.7	1,524.4
Jordan	170.5	0.08	16.9	18.8
Kazakhstan	365.7	0.17	—	72.6
Kenya	271.4	0.13	37.0	21.5
Kiribati	5.6	0.00	—	1.2
Korea	1,633.6	0.77	72.9	161.5
Kuwait	1,381.1	0.65	26.7	265.0
Kyrgyz Republic	88.8	0.04	—	18.9
Lao P.D.R.	52.9	0.02	9.4	2.1
Latvia	126.8	0.06	—	26.8
Lebanon	203.0	0.10	4.4	38.4
Lesotho	34.9	0.02	3.7	3.3
Liberia*	71.3	0.03	21.0	7.2
Libya	1,123.7	0.53	58.8	180.9
Lithuania	144.2	0.07	—	30.3
Luxembourg	279.1	0.13	17.0	22.8
Macedonia, F.Y.R. of	68.9	0.03	8.4	6.2
Madagascar	122.2	0.06	19.3	7.2
Malawi	69.4	0.03	11.0	3.9

IMF MEMBERSHIP, QUOTAS, AND ALLOCATIONS OF SDRs *(continued)*

Member	Quota	Quota Share	Existing SDR Cumulative Allocation	Proposed Special SDR Allocation[1]
Malaysia	1,486.6	0.70	139.0	105.1
Maldives	8.2	0.00	0.3	1.3
Mali	93.3	0.04	15.9	4.3
Malta	102.0	0.05	11.3	8.5
Marshall Islands	2.5	0.00	—	0.7
Mauritania	64.4	0.03	9.7	4.2
Mauritius	101.6	0.05	15.7	5.7
Mexico	2,585.8	1.22	290.0	224.0
Micronesia, Federated States of	5.1	0.00	—	1.0
Moldova	123.2	0.06	—	26.4
Mongolia	51.1	0.02	—	10.9
Morocco	588.2	0.28	85.7	39.7
Mozambique	113.6	0.05	—	24.6
Myanmar	258.4	0.12	43.5	10.7
Namibia	136.5	0.06	—	29.2
Nepal	71.3	0.03	8.1	7.1
Netherlands	5,162.4	2.43	530.3	479.4
New Zealand	894.6	0.42	141.3	49.3
Nicaragua	130.0	0.06	19.5	8.7
Niger	65.8	0.03	9.4	4.8
Nigeria	1,753.2	0.83	157.2	218.6
Norway	1,671.7	0.79	167.8	156.1
Oman	194.0	0.09	6.3	28.7
Pakistan	1,033.7	0.49	170.0	52.3
Palau	3.1	0.00	—	0.7
Panama	206.6	0.10	26.3	17.5
Papua New Guinea	131.6	0.06	9.3	18.6
Paraguay	99.9	0.05	13.7	7.4
Peru	638.4	0.30	91.3	45.3
Philippines	879.9	0.41	116.6	69.1
Poland	1,369.0	0.64	—	289.8
Portugal	867.4	0.41	53.3	110.1
Qatar	263.8	0.12	12.8	43.0
Romania	1,030.2	0.49	76.0	145.1
Russia	5,945.4	2.80	—	1,264.4

IMF MEMBERSHIP, QUOTAS, AND ALLOCATIONS OF SDRs *(continued)*

Member	Quota	Quota Share	Existing SDR Cumulative Allocation	Proposed Special SDR Allocation[1]
Rwanda	80.1	0.04	13.7	3.7
Samoa	11.6	0.01	1.1	1.3
San Marino	17.0	0.01	—	2.9
São Tomé and Príncipe	7.4	0.00	0.6	1.0
Saudi Arabia	6,985.5	3.29	195.5	1,308.5
Senegal	161.8	0.08	24.5	10.4
Seychelles	8.8	0.00	0.4	1.4
Sierra Leone	103.7	0.05	17.5	5.2
Singapore	862.5	0.41	16.5	88.4
Slovak Republic	357.5	0.17	—	75.5
Slovenia	231.7	0.11	25.4	18.7
Solomon Islands	10.4	0.01	0.7	1.5
Somalia*	44.2	0.02	13.7	4.2
South Africa	1,868.5	0.88	220.4	179.9
Spain	3,048.9	1.44	298.8	268.6
Sri Lanka	413.4	0.19	70.9	18.1
St. Kitts and Nevis	8.9	0.00	—	1.9
St. Lucia	15.3	0.01	0.7	2.5
St. Vincent and the Grenadines	8.3	0.00	0.4	1.4
Sudan*	169.7	0.08	52.2	16.1
Suriname	92.1	0.04	7.8	12.1
Swaziland	50.7	0.02	6.4	4.3
Sweden	2,395.5	1.13	246.5	226.6
Switzerland	3,458.5	1.63	—	724.2
Syrian Arab Republic	293.6	0.14	36.6	25.0
Tajikistan	87.0	0.04	—	17.6
Tanzania	198.9	0.09	31.4	11.7
Thailand	1,081.9	0.51	84.7	83.6
Togo	73.4	0.03	11.0	4.9
Tonga	6.9	0.00	—	1.5
Trinidad and Tobago	335.6	0.16	46.2	26.1
Tunisia	286.5	0.13	34.2	26.1
Turkey	964.0	0.45	112.3	75.9
Turkmenistan	75.2	0.04	—	14.1
Uganda	180.5	0.08	29.4	9.9

IMF MEMBERSHIP, QUOTAS, AND ALLOCATIONS OF SDRS *(concluded)*

Member	Quota	Quota Share	Existing SDR Cumulative Allocation	Proposed Special SDR Allocation[1]
Ukraine	1,372.0	0.65	—	292.4
United Arab Emirates	611.7	0.29	38.7	76.2
United Kingdom	10,738.5	5.06	1,913.1	260.6
United States	37,149.3	17.49	4,899.5	2,877.0
Uruguay	306.5	0.14	50.0	16.1
Uzbekistan	275.6	0.13	—	58.5
Vanuatu	17.0	0.01	—	3.7
Venezuela, Republica Bolivariana de	2,659.1	1.25	316.9	255.1
Vietnam	329.1	0.15	47.7	23.2
Yemen, Republic of	243.5	0.11	28.7	23.0
Yugoslavia, Fed. Rep. of (Serbia/Montenegro)	467.7	0.22	56.7	41.7
Zambia	489.1	0.23	68.3	38.3
Zimbabwe	353.4	0.17	10.2	66.4
Total	**212,414.9**	**100.00**	**21,433.3**	**21,434.0**

Note: Numbers may not add to totals due to rounding.

*These countries have not yet consented to their Ninth (November 11, 1992) or Eleventh (January 22, 1999) Review quota increases, except for the Islamic State of Afghanistan, which has not yet consented to the Eleventh Review but has consented to the Ninth Review. There were no increases in quotas under the Tenth Review.

[1]Special allocation of SDRs using a benchmark ratio of cumulative allocations to Ninth Review quotas of 29.315788813 percent. It includes the proposed special allocation for Palau, which became a member after September 19, 1997, and proposed allocations for members in arrears to the IMF, although their allocations will be held in escrow accounts until the arrears are cleared.

Appendix II

SPECIAL VOTING MAJORITIES FOR SELECTED FINANCIAL DECISIONS

Subject	Special Majority[1]	Article
Adjustment of quotas	85 percent	III, Sec. 2(c)
Medium of payment for increased quota	70 percent	III, Sec. 3(d)
Calculation of reserve tranche positions: exclusion of certain purchases and holdings	85 percent	XXX, Sec. (c)(iii)
Change in obligatory periods for repurchase	85 percent	V, Sec. 7(c), (d)
Determination of rates of charge or remuneration	70 percent	V, Sec. 8(d), 9(a)
Increase in percentage of quota for remuneration	70 percent	V, Sec. 9(c)
Sale of gold	85 percent	V, Sec. 12(b), (c), (e)
Acceptance of gold in payments to IMF	85 percent	V, Sec. 12(b), (d)
SDA assets		V, Sec. 12(f)
Transfer to GRA	70 percent	
Balance of payments assistance to developing members	85 percent	
Distribution from general reserve	70 percent	XII, Sec. 6(d)
Valuation of SDR		XV, Sec. 2
Fundamental change in principle	85 percent	
Other change	70 percent	
Allocation of SDRs	85 percent	XVIII, Sec. 4(d)
Determination of rate of interest on SDRs	70 percent	XX, Sec. 3
Prescription of official holders of SDRs	85 percent	XVII, Sec. 3
Suspension or reinstatement of voting rights	70 percent	XXVI, Sec. 2(b)
Compulsory withdrawal	85 percent	XXVI, Sec. 2(c)
Amendment of the IMF's Articles of Agreement	85 percent[2]	XXVIII (a)

[1]Proportion of total voting power.
[2]Three-fifths of the members having 85 percent of the voting power.

Appendix III

Other Administered Accounts

The IMF may establish administered accounts for purposes such as financial and technical assistance. Such accounts are legally and financially separate from all other accounts of the IMF.[1]

The role of the IMF as trustee has proved particularly useful in enabling the creation of mechanisms to:

- *reduce the cost of access for low-income developing member countries* to the facilities of the General Resources Account, as in the case of the Oil Facility Subsidy Account (1975–83) and the Supplementary Financing Facility Subsidy Account (1979–84);
- *provide balance of payments assistance on concessional terms*, as in the case of the Trust Fund (1976–81), the PRGF Trust (1987–), and several accounts administered by the IMF on behalf of individual members to provide contributions to the PRGF Subsidy Account; and
- *provide special financing to heavily indebted poor countries*, as in the case of the PRGF-HIPC Trust and the Umbrella Account for HIPC operations.

From time to time, the IMF also has decided to establish, on an ad hoc basis and as requested by members, other accounts for the administration of resources for several purposes. These are described below.

Administered Account Japan

At the request of Japan, the IMF established an account on March 3, 1989 to administer resources, made available by Japan or other countries with Japan's concurrence, that are to be used to assist certain members with overdue obligations to the IMF. The resources of the account are to be disbursed in amounts specified by Japan and to members designated by Japan.

---

[1]The legal authority of the IMF to act as an administrator of such resources derives from Article V, Section 2*(b)*, which empowers it, if requested, to "perform financial and technical services, including the administration of resources contributed by members, that are consistent with the purposes of the Fund." The operations involved in the performance of such financial services cannot "be on the account of the Fund."

173

Administered Account for Selected Fund Activities — Japan

At the request of Japan, the IMF established the Administered Technical Assistance Account — Japan on March 19, 1990 to administer resources contributed by Japan to finance technical assistance to member countries. On July 21, 1997, the account was renamed the Administered Account for Selected Fund Activities — Japan and amended to include the administration of resources contributed by Japan in support of the IMF's Regional Office for Asia and the Pacific (OAP). The resources of the account designated for technical assistance activities are used with the approval of Japan and include the provision of scholarships; the resources designated for the OAP are used as agreed between Japan and the IMF for certain activities of the IMF with respect to Asia and the Pacific through the OAP. Disbursements can also be made from the account to the General Resources Account to reimburse the IMF for qualifying technical assistance projects and OAP expenses.

Framework Administered Account for Technical Assistance Activities

The Framework Administered Account for Technical Assistance Activities ("the Framework Account") was established by the IMF on April 3, 1995 to receive and administer contributed resources that are to be used to finance technical assistance consistent with the purposes of the IMF. The financing of technical assistance activities is implemented through the establishment and operation of subaccounts within the Framework Account. The establishment of a subaccount requires the approval of the Executive Board. Resources are to be used in accordance with the written understanding between the contributor and the Managing Director. Disbursements can also be made from the Framework Account to the General Resources Account to reimburse the IMF for its costs incurred on behalf of technical assistance activities financed by resources from the Framework Account.

Subaccount for Japan Advanced Scholarship Program

At the request of Japan, this subaccount was established on June 6, 1995 to finance the cost of studies and training of nationals of member countries in macroeconomics and related subjects at selected universities and institutions. The scholarship program focuses primarily on the training of nationals of Asian member countries, including Japan.

Rwanda — Macroeconomic Management Capacity Subaccount

At the request of Rwanda, this subaccount was established on December 20, 1995 to finance technical assistance to rehabilitate and strengthen Rwanda's macroeconomic management capacity.

Australia — IMF Scholarship Program for Asia Subaccount

At the request of Australia, this subaccount was established on June 5, 1996 to finance the cost of studies and training of government and central bank officials in macroeconomic management so as to enable them to contribute to their countries' achievement of sustainable economic growth and development. The program focuses primarily on the training of nationals of Asian countries.

Switzerland Technical Assistance Subaccount

At the request of Switzerland, this subaccount was established on August 27, 1996 to finance the costs of technical assistance activities of the IMF that consist of policy advice and training in macroeconomic management.

French Technical Assistance Subaccount

At the request of France, this subaccount was established on September 30, 1996 to cofinance the costs of training in economic fields for nationals of certain member countries.

Denmark Technical Assistance Subaccount

At the request of Denmark, this subaccount was established on August 25, 1998 to finance the costs of technical assistance activities of the IMF that consist of advising on policy and administrative reforms in the fiscal, monetary, and related statistical fields.

Australia Technical Assistance Subaccount

At the request of Australia, this subaccount was established on March 7, 2000 to finance the costs of technical assistance activities of the

175

IMF that consist of advising on the design of policy and administrative reforms in the fiscal, monetary, and related statistical fields, as well as providing training in the formulation and implementation of macroeconomic and financial policies.

The Netherlands Technical Assistance Subaccount

At the request of the Netherlands, this subaccount was established on July 27, 2000 to finance projects that seek to enhance the capacity of members to formulate and implement policies in the macroeconomic, fiscal, monetary, financial, and related statistical fields, including training programs and projects that strengthen the legal and administrative framework in these core areas.

Administered Account—Spain

At the request of Spain, the IMF established an account on March 20, 2001 to administer resources up to $1 billion contributed by Spain for Argentina. The resources of this account are to be used to assist Argentina in the implementation of the adjustment program supported by the IMF under the Stand-By Arrangement for Argentina approved on March 10, 2000 and augmented on January 12, 2001.

Administered Account for Rwanda

At the request of the Netherlands, Sweden, and the United States ("the donor countries"), the IMF established an account on October 27, 1995 to administer resources contributed by the donor countries to provide grants to Rwanda. These grants are used for reimbursing the service charge and reducing, to the equivalent of a rate of ½ of 1 percent a year, the rate of the quarterly charges payable by Rwanda on its use of the IMF's financial resources under the Compensatory and Contingency Financing Facility. The account was terminated on November 30, 2000.

Trust Fund

The Trust Fund, for which the IMF is Trustee, was established in 1976 to provide balance of payments assistance on concessional terms to eligible members that qualify for assistance. In 1980, the IMF, as Trustee, decided that, upon the completion of the final loan disbursements, the Trust Fund would be terminated as of April 30, 1981, and after that date, the activities of the Trust Fund have been confined to receiving interest and repayments and transferring these receipts to the Special Disbursement Account of the General Department.

Supplementary Financing Facility Subsidy Account

The Supplementary Financing Facility Subsidy Account ("the Subsidy Account"), which is administered by the IMF, was established in December 1980 to assist low-income developing country members to meet the cost of using resources made available through the IMF's Supplementary Financing Facility and under the policy on exceptional use. All repurchases due under these policies were scheduled for completion by January 31, 1991, and the final subsidy payments were approved in July 1991. However, two members (Liberia and Sudan), overdue in the payment of charges, remain ineligible to receive previously approved subsidy payments until their overdue charges are settled. Accordingly, the account remains in operation and has retained amounts for payment to these members after the overdue charges are paid.

Post-Conflict Emergency Assistance
Subsidy Account for PRGF-Eligible Members

The IMF established an account on May 4, 2001 to administer resources contributed by members for the purpose of providing assistance to PRGF-eligible members in support of their adjustment efforts. Contributions to the account will be used to provide grants to PRGF-eligible members that have made purchases under the IMF's policy on post-conflict emergency assistance, effectively subsidizing the rate of charge on these purchases to 0.5 percent annually.

Appendix IV

Disclosure of Financial Position with the IMF in the Balance Sheet of a Member's Central Bank

This appendix elaborates on the final section of Chapter II in the text, "Disclosure of Financial Position with the IMF in the Member Country." The following four examples illustrate the gross and net methods for reporting IMF-related assets and liabilities in the balance sheet of a central bank that is acting both as the IMF's depository and fiscal agent.

In the examples below, all figures represent local currency units.

I. The basic underlying assumptions for Examples 1 and 2 are:

(a) On the balance sheet date, the member has a quota equal to 2 million in local currency and an SDR allocation of 1 million;

(b) The reserve tranche portion of the subscription (25 percent of the quota) has been paid in SDRs. Hence, the central bank's SDR holdings, originally equal to 1 million in local currency, are lower by 500,000 on the balance sheet date; and

(c) The member has elected to pay 99 percent of the local currency subscription (75 percent of its quota) in the form of nonnegotiable, non-interest-bearing securities. Of the remaining 1 percent (15,000), $9/10$ has been paid into the IMF No. 1 Account and $1/10$ is maintained in the No. 2 Account.

Example 1. Gross method

Balance Sheet

Assets		Liabilities	
Foreign assets:		*Foreign liabilities:*	
IMF quota	2,000,000	IMF No. 1 Account	13,500
		IMF No. 2 Account	1,500
		IMF Securities Account	1,485,000
		Total IMF currency holdings	1,500,000
SDR holdings	500,000	SDR allocation	1,000,000
Total assets	2,500,000	Total liabilities	2,500,000

Example 2. Net method

Balance Sheet

Assets		Liabilities	
Foreign assets:		*Foreign liabilities:*	
IMF reserve tranche position	501,500	IMF No. 2 Account	1,500
		Net SDR allocation	500,000
Total assets	501,500	Total liabilities	501,500

II. Additional assumptions for Examples 3 and 4 are:
   (d) The member has drawn its reserve tranche position of 500,000 in local currency; and
   (e) The member has received IMF resources (used IMF credit) equal to 4,500,000 for which securities have been issued.

Example 3. Gross method

Balance Sheet

Assets		Liabilities	
Foreign assets:		*Foreign liabilities:*	
IMF quota	2,000,000	IMF No. 1 Account	13,500
		IMF No. 2 Account	1,500
		IMF Securities Account	6,485,000
		Total IMF currency holdings[1]	6,500,000
SDR holdings	500,000	SDR allocation	1,000,000
Foreign reserves	5,000,000		
Total assets	7,500,000	Total liabilities	7,500,000

[1]Includes 4,500,000 in local currency stemming from the use of IMF credit and 500,000 from the drawing of the reserve tranche.

Example 4. Net method

Balance Sheet

Assets		Liabilities	
Foreign assets:		*Foreign liabilities:*	
Foreign reserves[1]	5,000,000	Use of IMF credit	4,500,000
		Net SDR allocation	500,000
Total assets	5,000,000	Total liabilities	5,000,000

[1]Foreign reserves are net of the balance in the No. 2 Account.

Glossary

This glossary covers basic operational and financial terms as used in the IMF. Words in light *italics* are "see also" references.

A

Access Policy and Access Limits. The IMF has established policies that govern the use of its resources by members and define the maximum amounts that can be borrowed from the IMF by member countries. A member country's access limits are set as percentages of the member's *quota* and vary with the facility being used; the limits are reviewed periodically. The access limits for drawings under the *credit tranches* (normally through *Stand-By Arrangements*) and under the *Extended Fund Facility* (normally through *Extended Arrangements*) have remained unchanged since 1994 — at 100 percent of quota annually and 300 percent of quota, cumulatively. The access limits under the three-year *Poverty Reduction and Growth Facility* arrangements are 140 percent of quota in normal circumstances and 185 percent of quota in exceptional circumstances. Access under the *Supplemental Reserve Facility* and *Contingent Credit Lines* is not subject to quota limits.

Accounting Unit. The IMF's unit of account in which its financial records are kept is the *special drawing right* (SDR). Members' currencies are valued by the IMF in terms of the SDR on the basis of their *representative rates* of exchange, normally against the U.S. dollar at spot market rates if available.

Accounts and Departments. The IMF operates its financial functions through the *General Department*, the *SDR Department*, and the *Administered Accounts*, which are accounting constructs and not organizational units. The financial functions of the IMF are discharged by the Treasurer's Department, which is an organizational unit of the staff.

Accounts of the IMF in Member Countries. The IMF's currency holdings are held in accounts of the IMF in designated *depositories* in member countries. These accounts are the No. 1 and No. 2 Accounts, and the Securities Account. The No. 1 Account is used for *quota* subscription payments, *purchases and repurchases*, repayment of borrowing, and sales of the member's currency. All these transactions may also be carried out through the Securities Account, which may be established by the member to hold nonnegotiable, non-interest-bearing notes, or similar obligations, payable to the IMF on demand. These notes or similar obligations are issued by the member as a substitute for the currency holdings of the IMF. The No. 2 Account is used for the IMF's administrative expenditures and receipts in the member's currency and within its territory.

Adequate Safeguards. Under the Articles, the IMF is to make its *general resources* temporarily available to members "under adequate safeguards." The IMF considers that the principal safeguard for repayment is a strong economic *adjustment program.* The IMF has also adopted specific measures to protect against misuse of IMF resources by ensuring that members have in place adequate accounting, reporting, and auditing systems and that they provide the IMF with timely, accurate, and comprehensive information. Other safeguards include IMF technical assistance, formal post-program monitoring, and codes and best practices relating to transparency, statistical reporting, and governance.

Adjustment Program. A detailed economic program, usually supported by use of IMF resources, that is based on an analysis of the economic problems of the member country and specifies the policies being implemented or that will be implemented by the country in the monetary, fiscal, external, and structural areas, as necessary, to achieve economic stabilization and set the basis for sustained economic growth.

Administered Accounts. Accounts established to perform financial and technical services that are consistent with the purposes of the IMF, including the administration of resources contributed by individual members to provide assistance to other members. All transactions involving the Administered Accounts are separate from those of the IMF's other accounts.

Amendments (to the Articles of Agreement). The *Articles of Agreement* have been amended three times. The First Amendment (July 1969) introduced the *special drawing right* (SDR). The Second Amendment (April 1978) reflected the change from the par value exchange system based on a fixed price for gold to an international monetary system permitting floating exchange rates. The Third Amendment (November 1992) allowed for the suspension of voting and certain related rights of a member that fails to fulfill any of its obligations under the Articles (other than obligations with respect to SDRs). The Board of Governors in September 1997 adopted a resolution to amend the Articles to allow for a special one-time allocation of SDRs. This proposed fourth amendment will become effective when three-fifths of membership having 85 percent of the total voting power have accepted it.

Arrangement. A decision by the IMF that gives a member the assurance that it stands ready to provide foreign exchange or SDRs in accordance with the terms of the decision during a specified period of time. An IMF arrangement—which is not a legal contract—is approved by the Executive Board in support of an *adjustment program.*

Articles of Agreement. An international treaty that sets out the purposes, principles, and financial structure of the IMF. The Articles, which entered into force in December 1945, were drafted by representatives of 45 nations at a conference held in Bretton Woods, New Hampshire.

B

Basic Period. Each of the consecutive periods of five years (or less) during which a determination is made whether there is a global need for additional international reserves to justify a new allocation of SDRs. There has not been any allocation since the Third Basic Period (1978–81).

Basic Rate of Charge. The interest charge that is applied to outstanding IMF credit financed from the IMF's *general resources.* The basic rate of charge, which is set as a proportion of the weekly *SDR interest rate*, is applied to the daily balance of all outstanding *purchases* (credit) during each of the IMF's financial quarters. The basic rate is subject to a *surcharge.*

Benchmark Bond Index. Under the IMF's investment strategy for the assets held for concessional assistance, the benchmark is a customized index comprising one- to three-year government bond indices for Germany, Japan, the United Kingdom, and the United States with each market weighted to reflect the currency composition of the SDR basket.

Benchmarks. In the context of IMF programs, a point of reference against which progress may be monitored. Benchmarks are not necessarily quantitative and frequently relate to structural variables and policies. Some benchmarks may be converted to *performance criteria*, required to be observed in order to qualify for phased borrowings. In addition, quantitative benchmarks are set for the quarters for which there are no performance criteria, and structural benchmarks may be set for any date.

Burden Sharing. A policy, under decisions adopted by the Executive Board of the IMF since 1986, regarding the sharing, between members paying *charges* and members receiving *remuneration*, of the financial consequences to the IMF of overdue obligations. An amount equal to overdue charges (excluding special charges) and an allocation to the *Special Contingent Account* are generated each quarter by an upward adjustment of the rate of charge and a downward adjustment of the rate of remuneration.

C

Charges, Periodic. Charges (interest) payable by a member on its outstanding use of IMF credit. Charges are normally levied quarterly (see *Basic Rate of Charge, Special Charges*).

Commitment Fee (Stand-By or Extended Arrangement Charge including amounts available under the Supplemental Reserve Facility and the Contingent Credit Line). A charge is payable at the beginning of each period (usually one year) on the resources committed for that period. This fee is refunded when committed resources are drawn.

Compensatory Financing Facility. A special IMF financing facility that provides resources to members who encounter balance of payments difficulties, arising out of export shortfalls or excess costs of cereal imports that are temporary and result from events that are largely beyond the members' control.

Conditionality. Economic policies that members intend to follow as a condition for the use of IMF resources. These are often expressed as *performance criteria* (e.g., monetary and budgetary targets) or *benchmarks*, are generally monitored through *program reviews*, and are intended to ensure that the use of IMF credit is temporary and consistent with the borrowing country's *adjustment program*.

Contingent Credit Line (CCL). The CCL is aimed at preventing the spread of a financial crisis, by enabling countries that are basically sound and well managed to put in place precautionary financing in case a crisis should occur. Short-term financing would be provided under a *Stand-By Arrangement* primarily to help members overcome the balance of payments financing needs arising from a sudden and disruptive loss of market confidence due to contagion, and largely generated by circumstances beyond the members' control.

Credit Tranche Policies. Policies under which members may make use of IMF credit to address general balance of payments problems. The credit tranche policies are distinct from special policies (facilities) the IMF has adopted to address special balance of payments problems. The amount of such use is related to a member's *quota*. Early in its history, the IMF made credit available in four tranches (segments), each equal to 25 percent of a member's quota. Provided a member is making reasonable efforts to solve its balance of payments problems, it can make use of IMF resources up to the limit of the first credit tranche on fairly liberal terms. Requests for use of more resources (in the upper credit tranches) require substantial grounds for expecting that the member's balance of payments difficulties will be resolved

184

within a reasonable period of time. Such use is almost always made under a *Stand-By Arrangement*, entailing *phasing* of purchases, *performance criteria*, and reviews — in other words, higher *conditionality*.

Creditor (or Reserve) Position in the IMF. A member has a creditor (or reserve) position in the IMF if it has lent its currency to the IMF under a loan agreement, and/or the member has not purchased its *reserve tranche* with the IMF, and/or the IMF has used the holdings of the member's currency — which were acquired by the IMF as part of the member's *quota* payment — to provide financial assistance to other members. More precisely, the creditor (or reserve) position is the sum of any outstanding borrowing by the IMF from the member and the member's *reserve tranche position*.

Cross Conditionality, Avoidance of. To avoid duplication of requirements by the IMF and the World Bank — known as cross-conditionality — there is an understanding that each institution must proceed with its own financial assistance according to the standards laid down in its respective *Articles of Agreement* and the policies adopted by its Executive Board. In other words, compliance with the requirements of one institution ought not be made a condition for the availability of financial assistance by the other institution. A country must, however, be a member of the IMF in order to join the World Bank.

Currency Holdings. The currency holdings of the IMF are the resources held at the disposal of the IMF in the IMF No. 1 Account, No. 2 Account, and Securities Account in its member countries, which are obtained as a result of members' *quota* payments and transactions between the IMF and members.

D

Depository and Fiscal Agency. Each member designates a fiscal agency (ministry of finance, central bank, or similar entity) to conduct financial transactions with the IMF and a depository (central bank or similar agency) to maintain the *accounts of the IMF* (the IMF No. 1 and No. 2 Accounts and the Securities Account). Each depository is required to pay out of the IMF's holdings of the member's currency, on demand and without delay, sums to any payee named by the IMF. The depository also holds for safe custody on behalf of the IMF nonnegotiable, non-interest-bearing notes, or similar instruments, issued by the member in substitution for part of the IMF's currency holdings.

Designation Plan. A list of participants in the *SDR Department* whose balance of payments and reserve positions are sufficiently strong for them to be called upon ("designated") to provide *freely usable currency* in exchange for SDRs within a financial quarter, together with the amounts they may be called upon to provide. The designation plan is established in advance of each financial quarter (currently only on a precautionary basis) by approval of the Executive Board.

E

Early (or Advance) Repurchase. A *repurchase* made before the end of the established maximum repurchase period. Under specific circumstances, the IMF may call upon a member to make an early repurchase.

Early Repurchase Expectation. The expectation of repurchase (repayment) in advance of its originally scheduled due date. According to the *Articles of Agreement*, a member is normally expected to repurchase its currency (make repayment of usable currencies) as its balance of payments and reserve positions improve. The IMF has also adopted early repayment schedules, pursuant to which members are expected to make repurchases of outstanding purchases in the credit tranches, under the *Compensatory Financing Facility* and the *Extended Fund Facility* earlier than the schedule of repurchase obligations. A separate early purchase expectation also applies to purchases made under the *Supplemental Reserve Facility* and the *Contingent Credit Lines.* Such repurchases are expected one year before they become due. At the request of the member, the IMF may decide to extend the expectation periods, though not beyond the due dates.

ELRIC. The five key areas of control and governance within a central bank that are considered for the adequacy of safeguards for IMF resources in assessments by the IMF are summarized under the acronym ELRIC as follows: *E*xternal audit mechanism, *L*egal structure and independence, financial *R*eporting, *I*nternal audit mechanism, and system of internal *C*ontrols.

Emergency Assistance. Since 1962, the IMF has provided emergency assistance in the form of *purchases* to help members overcome balance of payments problems arising from sudden and unforeseeable natural disasters. This assistance was extended in September 1995 to cover certain post-conflict situations. Assistance for post-conflict situations, as well as for natural disasters, is normally limited to 25 percent of quota, and in the case of post-conflict assistance, is available only if the member intends to move within a relatively short time to an upper *credit tranche* arrangement.

Emergency Financing Mechanism. A set of exceptional procedures to facilitate rapid Executive Board approval of IMF financial support for a member while ensuring the conditionality necessary to warrant such support. These emergency measures are used only in circumstances representing, or threatening to give rise to, a crisis in a member's external accounts that requires an immediate IMF response.

Enhanced Structural Adjustment Facility. A facility established in December 1987 to provide assistance on concessional terms to low-income member countries facing protracted balance of payments problems. In 1999, the facility was strengthened to make poverty reduction a key and more explicit focus, and its name was changed to the *Poverty Reduction and Growth Facility.*

Excluded Holdings. The part of a member's currency held in the General Resources Account that reflects the member's use of IMF credit and is therefore excluded when determining the member's *reserve tranche position* in the IMF. When determining a member's reserve tranche position, holdings in the IMF No. 2 Account that are less than $1/10$ of 1 percent of the member's quota also are excluded.

Extended Arrangement. An *arrangement* supported by resources under the *Extended Fund Facility.*

Extended Burden Sharing. The IMF established a second *Special Contingent Account (SCA-2)* on July 1, 1990, and decided to place SDR 1 billion to the account within about five years (through quarterly decreases to the rate of *remuneration* and increases to the *basic rate of charge*). These actions were taken to safeguard against possible losses arising from undischarged repurchase obligations related to purchases financed by the encashment of *"rights"* following the successful completion of a *rights accumulation program*. The SCA-2 was terminated in 1999. The balances in the account were refunded to the contributing members, many of whom chose to transfer these balances to the PRGF-HIPC Trust.

Extended Fund Facility. A financing facility under which the IMF supports medium-term economic programs that generally run for three years and are aimed at overcoming balance of payments difficulties resulting from macroeconomic and structural problems. Typically, an economic program states the general objectives for the three-year period and the specific policies for the first year; policies for subsequent years are spelled out in program reviews.

F

Financial Transactions Plan. The Executive Board adopts a financial transactions plan for each upcoming quarter specifying the amounts of SDRs and selected member currencies to be used in *purchases and repurchases* (transfers and receipts) expected to be conducted through the General Resources Account during that period.

First Credit Tranche Purchase. See *Credit Tranche Policies.*

Floating Facilities. *Purchases* (loans) under the special facilities, other than the *Extended Fund Facility* (currently the *Compensatory Financing Facility, emergency assistance*, and the *Supplemental Reserve Facility*, and the *Contingent Credit Line*), are not counted in calculating annual and cumulative access limits under the IMF's general policy on access limits. These are therefore termed "floating facilities" in terms of access to IMF resources. However, for the purpose of determining the level of conditionality (whether first tranche or higher), all purchases are taken into account.

Freely Usable Currency. A currency that the IMF has determined is widely used to make payments for international transactions and widely traded in the principal exchange markets. At present, the euro, Japanese yen, pound sterling, and U.S. dollar are classified as freely usable currencies.

G

General Arrangements to Borrow (GAB). Long-standing arrangements under which 11 industrial countries stand ready to lend to the IMF to finance *purchases* (loans) that aim at forestalling or coping with a situation that could impair the international monetary system. The GAB currently amount to SDR 17 billion, and there is also an associated agreement with Saudi Arabia for SDR 1.5 billion.

General Department. Comprises the General Resources Account, the Special Disbursement Account, and the Investment Account (not activated).

General Resources. Assets, whether *ordinary* (owned) or borrowed, maintained within the IMF's General Resources Account.

H

Heavily Indebted Poor Countries (HIPC) Initiative. The HIPC Initiative, adopted in 1996, provides exceptional assistance to eligible countries to reduce their external debt burdens to sustainable levels, thereby enabling them to service their external debt without the need for further debt relief and without compromising growth. The HIPC Initiative is a comprehensive approach to debt relief that involves multilateral, Paris Club, and other official and bilateral creditors. To ensure that debt relief is put to effective use, assistance under the HIPC Initiative is limited to PRGF- and IDA-eligible countries that have established a strong track record of policy implementation under PRGF- and IDA-supported programs. It is expected that as many as 36 IMF members could qualify for assistance under the enhanced HIPC Initiative (see below).

- *Eligibility.* A country must satisfy three criteria for HIPC assistance: (1) be eligible for concessional assistance from the IMF and World Bank; (2) face an unsustainable debt burden; and (3) establish a track record of reform and sound policies. All countries also must have adopted a Poverty Reduction Strategy Paper (PRSP) through a broad-based participatory process by the *decision point* and have made progress in implementing this strategy for at least one year by the *completion point* (see below).

- *Decision and Completion Points.* Under the HIPC framework, the IMF and the World Bank determine the eligibility of a member and the amount of HIPC assistance to be committed at the decision point—the point at which the member completes its first (typically three-year) record of good policy performance under programs supported by the IMF and the World Bank. Beginning from the decision point, an eligible member may receive interim assistance of up to 20 percent annually and 60 percent in total (25 percent and 75 percent, respectively, in exceptional circumstances) of the committed amount of HIPC assistance between the decision point and the completion point—the point when the member has fulfilled all policy-related conditions for HIPC assistance. Remaining undistributed HIPC Initiative assistance is delivered at the completion point.

- *Enhanced HIPC Initiative.* The original HIPC Initiative was modified and enhanced in 1999. The enhanced HIPC Initiative aims at providing deeper, faster, and broader debt relief to qualified members. Under this framework, the IMF and the World Bank determine the qualification of a member and the amount of HIPC assistance to be committed at the *decision point* (see above) of the program.

- *PRGF-HIPC Trust.* The Trust for Special PRGF Operations for the Heavily Indebted Poor Countries (HIPC) and Interim PRGF Operations. The trust was established in February 1997 to channel special assistance to eligible heavily indebted poor countries.

Holdings Rate. The exchange rate of a member's currency against the SDR, at which the IMF holds the currency of the member. The holdings rate is based on market exchange rates (see *accounting unit* and *representative rate*).

I

Interim Assistance. Beginning from the decision point under the *HIPC Initiative*, a qualified member may receive interim assistance of up to 20 percent annually and 60 percent in total (25 percent and 75 percent, respectively, in exceptional circumstances) of the committed amount in HIPC assistance between the decision point and the completion point.

Interim PRGF. The period between 2002 and 2005 is deemed the "interim" period since it is framed initially by the expected full commitment of loan resources available to the current PRGF Trust and subsequently by the intended initiation of operations under a *self-sustained PRGF.*

L

Liquidity Ratio. The ratio of the IMF's net uncommitted usable resources to its liquid liabilities. It is a measure of the IMF's lending capacity.

M

Maintenance of Value. See *Valuation Adjustment.*

Management Letter. Under IMF safeguards assessments, a letter issued by an external auditor to the management of a central bank that draws attention to material weaknesses in the internal control systems that have come to the attention of the auditor during the audit of financial statements (see *Safeguards*).

Medium-Term Instruments. Under the IMF's investment strategy, these instruments perform similarly to domestic government bonds, but are claims on the Bank for International Settlements (BIS) that offer liquidity and the possibility to benefit from a credit spread over domestic bonds.

Misreporting. The term misreporting is used broadly to cover situations in which a member provides incorrect information to the IMF.

N

Net Present Value (NPV). The NPV of debt is a measure that takes into account the degree of concessionality. It is the sum of all future debt-service obligations (interest and principal) on existing debt, discounted at the market interest rate. Whenever the interest rate on a loan is lower than the market rate, the resulting NPV of debt is smaller than its face value, with the difference reflecting the grant (concessionality) element.

New Arrangements to Borrow (NAB). Arrangements under which 25 member countries or their financial institutions stand ready to lend to the IMF under circumstances similar to those covered by the *General Arrangements to Borrow (GAB)*. The total amount of the NAB is SDR 34 billion, and the combined amount that can be drawn under the NAB and the GAB also cannot exceed SDR 34 billion.

Noncomplying Purchase. A *purchase* (loan) made under a *Stand-By* or an *Extended Arrangement* that the member is later found not entitled to have made — that is, the purchase was made on the basis of incorrect information. The IMF has a set of guidelines that apply in such cases and can call on the member to repay all or part of that purchase early (see also *Misreporting*).

O

Ordinary Resources. Assets held in the General Resources Account that derive from members' *quota* subscription payments and the undistributed net income from the use of these resources.

Outright Purchase. A *purchase* (loan) that is not made under any IMF arrangement.

P

Performance Criteria. Macroeconomic indicators such as monetary and budgetary targets, typically set on a quarterly basis, and, in some cases specific structural measures, for the member to qualify for purchases under the *phasing* schedule for *Stand-By Arrangements* in the upper credit tranches and for extended arrangements under the *Extended Fund Facility*; or on a typically six-month basis for disbursements under *Poverty Reduction and Growth Facility* Arrangements (see also *Benchmarks*).

Phasing. The practice of making the IMF's resources available to its members in installments over the period of an *arrangement*. The pattern of phasing can be even, front-loaded, or back-loaded, depending on the financing needs and the speed of adjustment.

Post-Program Monitoring. A formal safeguard measure introduced by the IMF in 2000 to monitor the economic performance of members whose *arrangements* have expired but who still have substantial IMF credit outstanding.

Poverty Reduction and Growth Facility (PRGF). Established as the *Enhanced Structural Adjustment Facility* in 1987, enlarged and extended in 1994, and further strengthened in 1999 to make poverty reduction a key and more explicit element. The purpose of the facility is to support *adjustment programs* to strengthen substantially and in a sustainable manner balance of payments positions, and to foster durable growth, leading to higher living standards and a reduction in poverty. Seventy-seven low-income countries are currently PRGF-eligible. Loans are disbursed under three-year arrangements, subject to observance of *performance criteria* and the completion of program reviews. Loans carry an annual interest rate of 0.5 percent, with a 5½-year grace period and a 10-year maturity.

- **Self-Sustained PRGF.** Under a self-sustained *Poverty Reduction and Growth Facility*, loans would not be financed by PRGF Trust borrowing (as under the current PRGF), but by IMF resources currently in the PRGF Trust Reserve Account, on a revolving basis. The self-sustained PRGF is expected to become effective around 2006.

Precautionary Arrangement. A *Stand-By* or an *Extended Arrangement* under which the member has indicated to the Executive Board its intention not to make *purchases*. Members may cease to treat an arrangement as precautionary at any time, and may make purchases thereunder as long as the conditions (performance criteria, reviews, etc.) under the arrangement have been met.

Precautionary Balances. Financial resources held in the form of General and Special Reserves and in the first *Special Contingent Account* established in the context of the arrears strategy for dealing with existing or potential overdue obligations.

Prescribed Holder. A nonparticipant in the *SDR Department* that has been prescribed by the IMF as a holder of SDRs, including nonmembers, member countries that are not *SDR Department* participants, institutions that perform the functions of a central bank for more than one member, and other official entities.

Program Monitoring. Monitoring by the IMF, including through the conduct of *program reviews*, to determine whether the *performance criteria* specified and policy commitments made in the context of a concurrent *Stand-By* or an *Extended Arrangement* are being observed by the member receiving resources. See also *post-program monitoring*.

Program Review. Provides a framework to assess progress on policies that cannot easily be quantified or defined as *performance criteria* and to assess overall progress toward program objectives of macroeconomic adjustment and structural reform in the context of an IMF program. The completion of a review makes available the next installment for purchases under the arrangement.

Protracted Arrears. Arrears to the IMF of more than six months.

Purchases and Repurchases. When the IMF makes its *general resources* available to a member, it does so by allowing the member to purchase SDRs or other members' currencies in exchange for its own (domestic) currency. The IMF's general resources are, by nature, revolving: purchases (loans) have to be reversed by repurchases (repayments) in installments within the period specified for a particular policy or facility. Although the purchase-repurchase mechanism is not technically or legally a loan, it is the functional equivalent of a loan.

Q

Quota. The capital subscription, expressed in SDRs, that each member must pay to the IMF on joining. Up to 25 percent is payable in SDRs or other acceptable reserve assets and the remainder in the member's own currency. Quotas, which reflect members' relative size in the world economy, are normally reviewed and possibly adjusted every five years.

R

Rebalancing of Portfolio. Portfolio rebalancing ensures that the currency composition of the investment portfolio managed by the IMF matches as closely as practicable the currency composition of the SDR basket.

Remunerated Reserve Tranche Position. The IMF pays interest, called *remuneration*, on a member's *reserve tranche position* except on a small portion that is provided to the IMF as interest-free resources. This unremunerated (non-interest-bearing) portion of the reserve tranche position is equal to 25 percent of the member's quota on April 1, 1978—that part of the quota that was paid in gold prior to the Second Amendment of the IMF's Articles. The gold tranche was never remunerated historically, so it was natural to set aside this same amount in terms of SDRs on this date as the unremunerated reserve tranche. For a member that joined the IMF after that date, the unremunerated reserve tranche is the same percentage of its initial quota as the average unremunerated reserve tranche was as a percentage of the quotas of all other members when the new member joined the IMF. The unremunerated reserve tranche remains fixed for each member in nominal terms, but because of subsequent quota increases, it is now significantly lower when expressed as a percentage of quota. At the present time, the average is equal to 3.8 percent of quota, but the actual percentage is different for each member.

Remuneration. The interest paid by the IMF every quarter on a member's *remunerated reserve tranche position*.

Representative Rate. The exchange rate of a member's currency, normally against the U.S. dollar, that is used in the IMF's *transactions* with that member — that is, a currency (other than the U.S. dollar) is valued in terms of the SDR in accordance with the value of the U.S. dollar in SDR terms and the representative rate of the other currency in terms of the U.S. dollar. If the member has an exchange market where a representative spot rate for the U.S. dollar (against the member's currency) can be readily ascertained, then that representative rate will be used. If such a market rate cannot be readily ascertained for the U.S. dollar but can be ascertained for another currency for which a representative market rate against the U.S. dollar exists, then that cross rate can be used. Otherwise, the IMF determines a rate for the currency that is appropriate.

Reserve Tranche Position. The member's *quota* less the IMF's holdings of a member's currency in the General Resources Account (excluding holdings that reflect the member's use of IMF credit and holdings in the IMF No. 2 Account that do not exceed $1/10$ of 1 percent of the member's quota). The reserve tranche position in the IMF is a part of the member's external reserves.

Rights Accumulation Program. An economic program agreed between the IMF and an eligible member in protracted arrears to the IMF that provides a framework for the member to establish a satisfactory track record of policy and payments performance, and permits the member to accumulate rights to future drawings of IMF resources following its clearance of arrears to the IMF up to the level of arrears outstanding at the beginning of the program.

Rights Approach. A special approach to address the situation of members that were in protracted arrears to the IMF at end-1989, on the basis of a *rights accumulation program*.

S

Safeguards. The IMF's Articles of Agreement stipulate that the IMF make its general resources temporarily available to members "under adequate safeguards." The principal safeguards used by the IMF are limits on access to appropriate amounts of financing, with incentives to contain excessively long or heavy use; conditionality and program design; safeguards assessments of central banks; and measures to deal with misreporting, supplemented by post-program monitoring and various voluntary activities, including the transparency (international standards and codes of good practice) and good governance initiatives.

Safeguards Assessment. An evaluation of a member country central bank's control, accounting, reporting and auditing systems to ensure that resources, including those provided by the IMF, are adequately monitored and controlled. The first stage determines whether there are clear vulnerabilities in these systems, based on information provided by central banks. If weaknesses in internal procedures are suspected, a second stage comprises on-site evaluations and recommendations for improvements. Safeguards assessments for all new users of IMF resources began after mid-year 2000 and will continue on an experimental basis until the policy is reviewed by the Executive Board in 2002. (See also *ELRIC*, *Stage One*, *Stage Two*, and *Transitional Procedures*.)

Service Charge. A fixed charge of ½ of 1 percent levied on each *purchase* of IMF resources in the General Resources Account other than *reserve tranche* purchases, which carry no charges. The service charge is payable at the time of the transaction.

Special Charges (Additional Charges). Charges in addition to the *basic rate of charge* levied on a member's overdue repurchases and charges.

Special Contingent Account. An account established to hold *precautionary balances* in order to strengthen the IMF's financial position in connection with members' overdue financial obligations.

Special Drawing Right (SDR). International reserve asset created by the IMF in 1969 as a supplement to existing reserve assets.

- **SDR Allocation.** Distribution of SDRs to members by decision of the IMF. A "general" allocation requires a finding by the IMF that there is a global need for additional liquidity.

- **SDR Assessment.** An assessment levied by the IMF, at the same rate for all participants in the *SDR Department*, on a participant's cumulative SDR allocations, to cover the expenses of conducting the business of the *SDR Department*.

- **SDR Department.** This department, an accounting entity rather than an organizational unit of the IMF, administers and records all transactions and operations involving SDRs.

- **SDR Interest and Charges.** Interest is paid to each holder of SDRs. Charges are levied, at the same rate, on each participant's cumulative SDR allocation. The SDR interest rate is determined weekly by reference to a combined market interest rate. Interest on SDR holdings is paid and charges on cumulative allocations are collected on a quarterly basis, and are settled on the first day of the subsequent quarter.

- **SDR Use.** Participants in the *SDR Department* (currently all members of the IMF) and *prescribed holders* may use SDRs in a variety of voluntary transfers, including transactions by agreement, swap arrangements, and forward operations. Participants may also use SDRs in transactions involving the General Resources Account of the IMF, such as the payment of charges (interest) and repurchases (repayments) of currencies. In addition, the IMF ensures that a participant with a need because of its balance of payments or reserve position is able to use its SDRs to acquire foreign exchange in a "transaction with designation" (see *Designation Plan*).

- **SDR Valuation.** The currency value of the SDR is determined daily by the IMF by summing the values in U.S. dollars, based on market exchange rates, of a basket of major currencies (the U.S. dollar, euro, Japanese yen, and pound sterling). The SDR valuation basket is normally reviewed and adjusted every five years.

Stage One. Under the IMF's *Safeguards Assessments*, this stage refers to a preliminary assessment of the adequacy of the central bank's *ELRIC* based on a review of documentation provided by the authorities and, if necessary, discussions with the external auditors.

Stage Two. Under the IMF's *Safeguards Assessments*, this stage refers to an on-site assessment mission that may be undertaken to confirm or modify the preliminary conclusions drawn by the *Stage One* assessment and propose specific remedial measures to alleviate confirmed vulnerabilities in a central bank's *ELRIC*.

Stand-By Arrangement. A decision of the IMF by which a member is assured that it will be able to make *purchases* from the General Resources Account up to a specified amount and during a specified period of time, usually one to two years, so long as the member observes the terms specified. Drawings under a Stand-By Arrangement are normally subject to *credit tranche policies*.

Supplemental Reserve Facility. A special facility established in December 1997 to provide financial assistance to members experiencing exceptional balance of payments difficulties due to short-term financing needs resulting from a sudden and disruptive loss of market confidence reflected in pressure on the capital account and the members' reserves.

Surcharge to the Basic Rate of Charge. A surcharge of 100 basis points is added to the *basic rate of charge* on outstanding IMF credit in excess of 200 percent of quota, and the surcharge rises to 200 basis points on credit above 300 percent of quota. The surcharge does not apply to purchases under the *Compensatory Financing Facility* and the special policy on *emergency assistance*. Different surcharges apply to credits under the *Contingent Credit Lines* and the *Supplemental Reserve Facility*.

Surveillance. An essential aspect of the IMF's responsibilities associated with overseeing the policies of its members, as specified in the *Articles of Agreement*, in order to ensure the effective operation of the international monetary system.

T

Transactions by Agreement. Transactions in which participants in the *SDR Department* (currently all IMF members) and/or *prescribed holders* voluntarily exchange SDRs for currency at the official rate as determined by the IMF.

Transitional Procedures. Under the IMF's *Safeguards Assessments*, these procedures are applicable to member countries with IMF arrangements in effect prior to June 30, 2000 and are similar to a *Stage One* assessment, except that the central bank is subject to assessment in only one area of the safeguards framework, namely the external audit mechanism.

U

Upper Credit Tranche. See *Credit Tranche Policies*.

Usable Currency. The currency of a member that the IMF considers is in a sufficiently strong external position that its currency can be used to finance IMF transactions with other members through the *financial transactions plan*. Not to be confused with *freely usable currency*.

Use of IMF Resources (or IMF Credit). Includes use of IMF resources under the General Resources Account, and loans made to members from the Special Disbursement Account or resources borrowed by the IMF as Trustee for the PRGF Trust. The use of IMF resources (or IMF credit) in the General Resources Account consists of transactions in which a member in need of balance of payments assistance uses its own currency to acquire from the IMF SDRs or the currency of a member in a strong balance of payments and reserve position. As a result of these transactions, the value in terms of SDRs of the IMF's aggregate holdings of SDRs and currencies do not change, but the composition of those holdings changes. The "strong" member whose currency is used to provide assistance sees a decrease in the IMF's holdings of its currency, while gaining an increased "reserve tranche position," on which it will receive *remuneration* or interest (unless the IMF's holdings of its currency remain within the unremunerated portion of the member's reserve tranche), and the IMF's holdings of the purchasing (borrowing) member's currency increases.

V

Valuation Adjustment. Each member has the obligation of maintaining the value in terms of the SDR of the balances of its currency held by the IMF. Whenever the holdings of a member's currency are revalued (for a "strong" member, typically when its currency is used in a transaction; for all members, at the end of the IMF's financial year), a receivable (for the IMF) or a payable (by the IMF) is established for the amount of currency payable by or to the member as a result of changes in the value of the currency against the SDR.

Value Date. The date on which the IMF establishes, in SDR terms, the value of a transaction. The IMF normally operates on a three-day value basis; that is, the value of the transaction is established on the basis of the exchange rate prevailing three business days before the transfer of funds actually takes place. However, if circumstances require it, the IMF can operate on a shorter value date.

Index

Page references in italics refer to tables and figures